Printed in the United States of America

First Printing, 2015

ISBN 978-0-692-44484-9

Book Print On Demand
PO Box 26287
Colorado Springs, CO 80936

www.bookprintondemand.com

DEDICATION

I would like to dedicate the book "Interrupted by God" to my family: my wife, Carol, my son Jesse, and my daughters Sarah, Naomi and Lydia who have helped me so much with my interruption by God.

The Immediate Family of David A. Quam
Naomi & Family Jesse & Family Sarah & Family Lydia & Family

Carol Dianne Quam (David's wife)

ACKNOWLEDGEMENTS

I will always be grateful to my three editors who helped me write the book "Interrupted By God": Amy Pavlo, Sarah Louise Quam Peterson and Tammie Hall.

TABLE OF CONTENTS

INTRODUCTION   7

PRELUDE   11

CHAPTER 1 – BIBLICAL CHARACTERS: OLD/NEW TESTAMENT   17

CHAPTER 2 – CHRISTIAN LEADERS PAST AND PRESENT   31

CHAPTER 3 – TESTIMONIES BY FAMILY AND FRIENDS   39

CHAPTER 4 – HISTORY OF THE MENNONITES   67

CHAPTER 5 – JACOB ALVIN SCHMIDT   77

CHAPTER 6 – THE LIFE OF ANDREW LEWIS QUAM   91

CHAPTER 7 – WHO IS GOD?   97

POSTLUDE   105

INTRODUCTION

Interruptions. No matter your station in life, education level, career, gender nor race will get you out of interruptions. All of us deal with them on a daily basis. Some of these, of course, are small. But many are huge—even life–changing. <u>Interruptions bring to the surface our true character</u>.

Any parent would testify that children account for a myriad of interruptions. Some may be small, but for the most part, interruptions from children are normal and teach parents patience. Sometimes the pleas from children seem to drive parents "up the wall."

What about the corporate employee, whether it be the CEO in a big office with the door propped open, the administrative assistant with multiple phone lines to answer or the busy person in a cubicle where distractions abound? How do people actually get things done at work?

Students in school get interrupted by fire drills, assemblies, disruptive students or even transitions to other subjects just when they are getting "in the groove" with a new concept or challenge.

In today's world, we deal with countless interruptions from media. You name it: Facebook, Twitter, Pinterest, Tumblr, text messaging, phone calls and emails that beg to be looked at and answered the second we receive them. Consider the "24 hour world" in which we live. People use their computers to bank, shop, research, chat, surf and SKYPE during every single hour of the day or night! The list goes on ad infinitum.

These are all fairly ordinary interruptions. But, what about the huge interruptions in life — those that change the course of our lives? A dire diagnosis from the doctor, a tragic accident, a lost job, a divorce lawyer calling, a child sent to the intensive care unit. These are the interruptions that we dread, pray against and hope will never happen.

But as we all know, these do happen, often more than we think they will. How do we handle them? Is our first reaction to say, "Why me?", "Why would God let this happen?", "This isn't fair!", or "He or she is such a great person—how could this tragedy occur?" We are all human and these are our natural reactions.

It is during these times, more often than not, that our Heavenly Father captures our attention. During tragedies a333nd traumas, we may start to pray like we've never prayed before and search God's word for His wisdom. We may start reaching out to those around us with our needs instead of thinking we've got it all together. During the worst times in life, we call upon God and fall into His arms because that is all we can do when our world is falling apart.

Countless people through the ages have encountered huge interruptions. Understanding how they handled them can help guide us. Consider all the biblical characters whose lives were Interrupted by God, including Abraham, Job, Daniel and King David to name just a few.

Consider Corrie Ten Boom, who survived the Holocaust, Fanny Crosby living with blindness, C. S. Lewis, who embraced Christ's truth after living as an atheist and Joni Eareckson Tada, who is an artist, author and speaker despite an accident that left her a paraplegic. Their lives were not only interrupted by the circumstances God allowed, they were transformed— and always for a greater end, a higher calling and a life closer to Jesus.

Consider how your life has been interrupted and what the results were. Did you turn to God or away from Him? Did you change for the better or become bitter? Do you have hope that God works in all things to show there are good and true purposes in His plan? Or have you become discouraged and feel beat–up?

Take courage for there is hope. Read on and encounter the faithful (while truly human and imperfect) who have learned that life's interruptions are not always what they seem. Be encouraged that God does know what He is doing. Especially when we do not!

PRELUDE

"A person's name is to that person the sweetest and most important sound in any language." I believe that truth as spoken by Dale Carnegie, because on January 16, 2007, I could not remember my own name. **God interrupted my life with a stroke on that day**. I was air–lifted via helicopter from Britton, South Dakota, to Fargo, North Dakota. I spent twelve days convalescing at Meritcare Hospital in Fargo and another month in an apartment across the river in Moorhead, Minnesota.

At 8pm on January 16, 2007, I was watching *The Honeymooners* (the black and white TV show starring Jackie Gleason) on DVD. I felt nothing was wrong. I had concluded a busy day as an interim pastor of the Rose Hill Evangelical Free Church near Langford in rural South Dakota, where I served for a year–and–a–half. At that point, I had lost 25 pounds by lifting weights, walking for an hour a day and dieting. I had just presented a sermon based on 1 Samuel 7 called, "Diet Theology." I was in good shape and I was feeling well. I even took time to play the Sheriff in a melodrama in Sisseton, SD. So I was surprised that evening in front of the TV.

Suddenly, I felt a sensation in my right wrist that lasted for about 2 seconds. I felt confused and was unable to speak. I knew I was having a stroke and the experience was surreal. I remember feeling helpless. But I was able to hurry to my wife, Carol, who was talking on the phone to Audrey Smeins, who is a nurse. My wife realized something was wrong because I could not speak, but I was gesturing like I wanted to go somewhere. My wife asked me if I was having a stroke. Audrey heard our conversation, and because of her experience as a nurse, she recognized the symptoms.

My wife drove approximately 75 miles per hour and brought me to the hospital in Britton, SD, which was 20 miles away. When we arrived at the hospital, several members of the congregation had already arrived and were gathering to pray. I found out later that Carol had called Bonnie Jensen and she had put the word out or the congregation to go to prayer. Bonnie and her husband, Herb (a farmer and rancher in the area), lived down the road from the parsonage.

It's the central nervous system that is threatened by a stroke. The term stroke is being replaced by "brain attack." A stroke is a disturbance of the brain due to an interruption of the flow of the blood supply.

At the hospital that night, I was aware of the fact that I was going to be air–lifted by helicopter to the hospital in Fargo, ND. As the helicopter sailed into the dark sky to the north, Donovan Jensen (a board member) remembers looking out the window of the Britton hospital and watching me go.

I remember the cold month of February 2007, after my stroke occurred living in an apartment convalescing. I remember taking multiple baths during the night. I do not know why I did this. My record was five baths within 24 hours. The effects of my stroke were numerous. For example, I forgot how to tie my necktie, how to whistle and how to distinguish my right hand from my left hand. I experienced unusual outbursts of laughing and crying. Although I did not experience any paralysis after my stroke, my speech was affected. The technical terms regarding my affected speech are aphasia and apraxia. Aphasia is word–find difficulty. This involves not remembering a word choice such as screwdriver. A stroke overcomer will know what the tool is used for, but not remember the actual word. The second term is apraxia, which causes the stroke overcomer to say the word 'screwdriver' incorrectly, perhaps something like "drew writer."

Recovering from a stroke is like swimming upstream. The road to overcoming my stroke was a long one, and God's grace was showered upon me during my recovery. My family helped me immensely. I was able to finish out my time as pastor of Rose Hill Evangelical Free Church in Langford, SD. My wife, Carol, wrote out my sermons in long hand as I dictated them. Then I would practice delivering the sermons as part of my speech therapy. The congregation at Rose Hill was gracious and I am grateful I was able to finish my time as pastor there.

David portraying a sheriff in a melodrama six months prior to the stroke

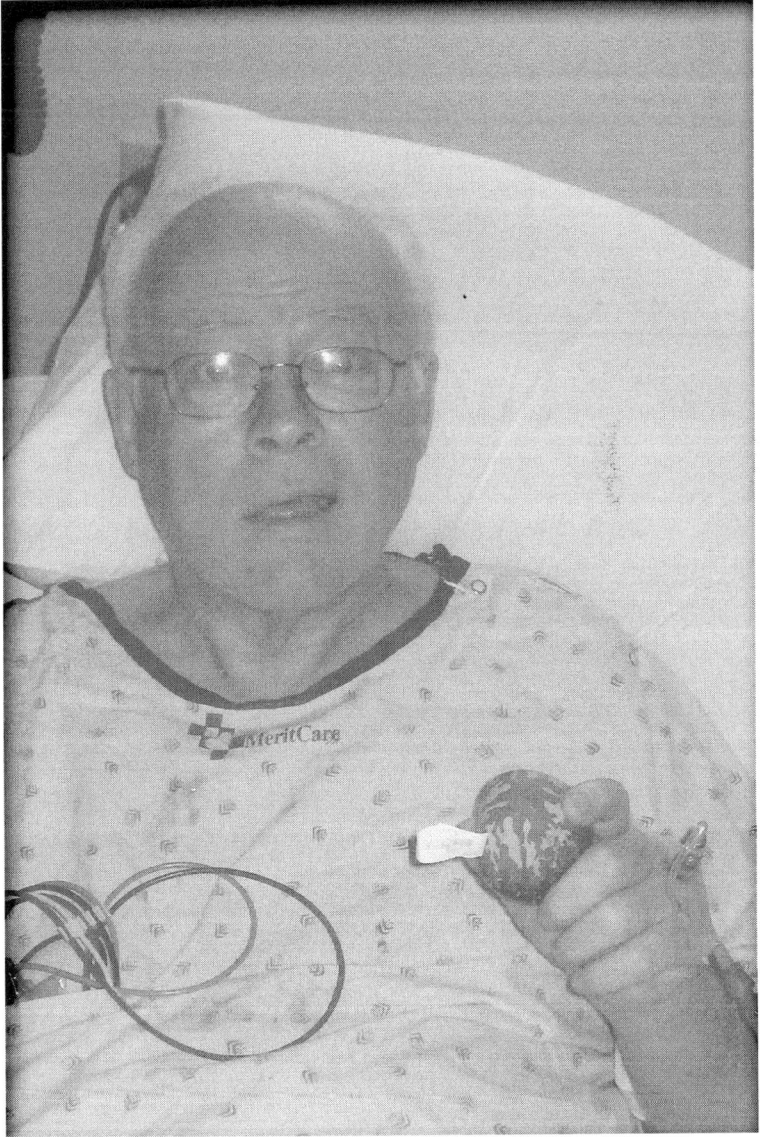

David after the stroke in hospital bed

CHAPTER 1

BIBLICAL CHARACTERS: OLD/NEW TESTAMENT

It is certainly true that a person's character is often revealed in how he or she handles interruptions. We can learn valuable lessons from the way in which the following biblical characters handled interruptions that God allowed in their lives. We will begin with the Old Testament.

ENOCH

"So all the days of Enoch were three hundred and sixty–five years. And Enoch walked with God; and he was not, for God took him."
Genesis 5:23–24

"By faith Enoch was taken away so that he did not see death, "and was not found, because God had taken him"; for before he was taken he had this testimony, that he pleased God." *Hebrews 11:5*

The taking away of Enoch has always been a mystery to me, as has the way Elijah was taken up to heaven (caught up in a chariot of clouds). Both of these men escaped death. I have heard a few sermons about Enoch, each of them focusing on what it means to truly walk with God. It is the desire of my heart to walk with God each and every day of my life.

Enoch was interrupted by God by being taken up to heaven quickly and in a miraculous way.

NOAH

"So the Lord said, "I will destroy man whom I have created from the face of the earth, both man and beast, creeping thing and birds of the air, for I am sorry that I have made them." But Noah found grace in the eyes of the Lord." *Genesis 6:7–8*

"By faith Noah, being divinely warned of things not yet seen, moved with godly fear, prepared an ark for the saving of his household, by which he condemned the world and became heir of the righteousness which is according to faith." *Hebrews 11:7*

Noah preached for 120 years and escaped the flood.

Think of it: Only Noah and his family were saved from the flood. I have heard many sermons about Noah, but I have noticed that while they answered questions about the flood, they have also raised few more questions.

Noah was interrupted by God because of a flood.

ABRAHAM

"...For we say that faith was accounted to Abraham for righteousness."
Romans 4:9

Abraham was not called by God until he was 75 years old and yet he obeyed God completely for the rest of his life. I must say that I have heard far too many sermons about Abraham! His life does, however, provide us with extraordinary examples of faith in action that we would do well to imitate. Abraham followed God's call to move from his home to a place he had never heard of. Then he waited with his wife, Sarah (who was barren) for a child of promise that would start the nation of Israel, God's chosen people. By God's miraculous power, Sarah did give birth to Isaac, the child of promise, when she was very old. Finally, Abraham was willing to sacrifice that same son to God when asked. God, of course, spared Abraham's son, Isaac, and Abraham's descendants are indeed "I will multiply your descendants as the stars of the heaven and as the sand which is on the seashore." *Genesis 22:17*

Abraham was interrupted by God when he took a radical journey into the unknown.

JACOB

"...Come, and let us go up to the mountain of the Lord, To the house of the God of Jacob;

He will teach us His ways, And we shall walk in His paths..." *Isaiah 2:3a*

This biblical character lied to his father and wrestled with God.

I am convinced that the reason we don't like to preach about Jacob's life is that we can't bear to look at ourselves in the mirror. In other words, when we look at Jacob's life, it reminds us of our failings. That is difficult for us, so we tend to shy away from Jacob's story.

He was the father of a dysfunctional family. He wrestled with God and he was never the same. The experience of wrestling with God brought about great change in Jacob's life. It brought him from a place of rebellion to a place of submission.

Jacob was interrupted by God via a wrestling match with the Creator of the universe.

JOSEPH (OLD TESTAMENT)

"The Lord was with Joseph, and he was a successful man; and he was in the house of his master the Egyptian. 3 And his master saw that the Lord was with him and that the Lord made all he did to prosper in his hand." *Genesis 39:2–3*

"...you meant evil against me; but God meant it for good..." *Genesis 50:20*

The interruption of Joseph's life brought him from a painful existence as a slave (after his brothers sold him to Egyptian slave traders) to that of becoming the prime minister of Egypt.

Joseph is one of my favorite Old Testament character because of the vast amount of material for sermons his life provides. A great question remains: How did Joseph move from such a dysfunctional experience in his family of origin to a life of devoted service to God? He excelled as the prime minister of Egypt and saved that country from starvation due to his shrewd planning as guided by God. He was a master at interpreting dream – a gift that also came from God. Joseph forgave his brothers for the horrible way they treated him and provided for them and their families with provisions and a home in Egypt.

Joseph's life was a miracle because God made him a "diamond in the rough" by delivering him from a truly dysfunctional home life. His father, Jacob, had 12 sons in 11 years by four different wives. Jacob favored Joseph above his other sons and great strife was present in his family.

Joseph was a picture of Christ in the New Testament.

Joseph was interrupted by God, who gave him two prophetic dreams that radically changed his life.

MOSES

"By faith Moses, when he became of age, refused to be called the son of Pharaoh's daughter, choosing rather to suffer affliction with the people of God than to enjoy the passing pleasures of sin, esteeming the reproach of Christ greater riches than the treasures in Egypt; for he looked to the reward." *Hebrews 11:24–26*

The public life of Moses started at age 80, with a burning bush, and ended with angels serving as pallbearers at his burial.

I heard a preacher give this synopsis of the life of Moses: God took Moses from being a "somebody" for 40 years (a favored adopted son in Egypt) to being a "nobody" for 40 year when he was a shepherd in the desert. But in His grace, God took this "nobody" and made him a great "somebody" in the last 40 years of his life as Moses led the nation of Israel, God's people.

Of all the biblical characters, Moses wins the prize for having the most interruptions in his life. Moses had succeeded in leading a group of (approximately 2–4 million) "chronic malcontents" through a vast desert over the span of 40 years. Under his leadership, the Israelites were guided from a path of disobedience to that of obedience to God's laws, the fulfillment of which was their entrance into the Promised Land.

Moses was interrupted by God who spoke to him from a burning bush.

JOB

"There was a man in the land of Uz, whose name was Job; and that man was blameless and upright, and one who feared God and shunned evil." *Job 1:1*

"And he said: Naked I came from my mother's womb, And naked shall I return there. The Lord gave, and the Lord has taken away; Blessed be the name of the Lord. In all this Job did not sin nor charge God with wrong." *Job 1:21–22*

Job was truly a suffering servant of God. Job suffered physically, mentally and spiritually. He courageously and tenaciously endured unimaginable suffering, yet he continued to trust and praise God. Job was described as "the greatest man among all the people of the East." In *Job 1:3b*. Yet God gave permission to Satan to test Job almost beyond what any human could bear. Job's six children were killed and his livestock were all destroyed. Job experienced horrific physical suffering and a deep trial of his faith in God. Even though God never revealed to Job why he suffered, God showed Job God's power, wisdom and character. In the last few s chapters of the book of Job in the Bible, God asks Job a series of 77 questions, including, "Where were you when I laid the foundations of the earth?" in *Job 38:4a*.

In *Job 40:4–5*, we see Job's response to God "Behold, I am vile; what shall I answer You? I lay my hand over my mouth. Once I have spoken, but I will not answer; Yes, twice, but I will proceed no further."

Ultimately, Job was able to believe that God was indeed Who He said He was. Job's life was restored to one that included more children, more property and better health after he endured the suffering. In the final chapter of Job, we read this: "Now the Lord blessed the latter days of Job more than his beginning." *Job 42:12a*

Job was interrupted by God through excruciating suffering.

JONAH

Jonah ran from God and was swallowed by a big fish.

He disobeyed God's instructions, asked to be thrown from the ship he was traveling on and was swallowed by a big fish. Jonah prayed from the belly of the fish, crying out to God in repentance.

The second time he was called by God, Jonah obeyed and presented God's truth to the people of Nineveh, who repented and thus their lives were transformed by God.

"For as Jonah was three days and three nights in the belly of the great fish, so will the Son of Man be three days and three nights in the heart of the earth." *Matthew 12:40*

Jonah was interrupted by God via a giant fish.

DANIEL

Daniel lived an uncompromising life.

A captive of the people of Babylon as a teenager, Daniel was led by God to refrain from eating the exotic food of the Babylonian king that had been sacrificed to idols. He obeyed God rather than man by ignoring the king's edict regarding prayer. Daniel still prayed to the One true God faithfully. For this he was thrown into a den of lions. God shut the mouths of the lions and miraculously protected Daniel. From this experience came the acknowledgement from Darius, the king of Babylon, of Jehovah God's power and reign.

The book of Daniel was written to encourage the exiled Jews. His writing combined with the book of Revelation gives an account for things to come. Just like Joseph he was an interpreter of dreams.

Daniel was interrupted by God when he was taken from his family to be a captive in Babylon.

DAVID

David served God as a young shepherd yet was chosen by Him to be the great king of the nation of Israel, God's people.

David was the quintessential man of God, yet he made many mistakes. He was a poor father, an average husband, an adulterer and a murderer. Yet God, in His mercy and sovereignty, used David to write numerous Psalms and to serve as Israel's king. David then paved the way for his son, Solomon, to build the temple of God. It is incredible that God in His grace called David a man after his own heart.

David was interrupted by God when he was chosen to be a king over Israel.

ESTHER

The biblical book of Esther doesn't contain the Name of God, nor prayer or sacrifice. Yet it is crystal clear in its narrative that God was in control of every event that touched Esther's life. She was a Jew summoned to be the wife of King Ahasuerus. When the evil Haman, who served in the king's court, hatched a plot to kill all of the Jewish people, Esther was bold enough to approach the king with wisdom and he in turn saved her people from death. Haman was hung for his crimes. Esther's uncle, Mordecai, counseled Esther as she appealed to the king.

Esther was interrupted by God by becoming a queen.

ELISHA

I have heard many sermons about Elijah but few on Elisha. But Elisha had a dramatic interruption by God. Just as Elijah resembled Moses, so Elisha resembled Joshua.

"So he departed from there, and found Elisha the son of Shaphat, who was plowing with twelve yoke of oxen before him, and he was with the twelfth. Then Elijah passed by him and threw his mantle on him...So Elisha turned back from him, and took a yoke of oxen and slaughtered them and boiled their flesh, using the oxen's equipment, and gave it to the people, and they ate. Then he arose and followed Elijah, and became his servant." *1 Kings 19:19, 21*

Elisha had twice as many recorded miracles than Elijah.

Elisha was interrupted by God when Elijah threw his mantle on Elisha and he burned his plow and hosted a farewell feast for his family and friends.

NEHEMIAH

I preached through the book of Nehemiah in the year 2006, prior to my stroke. I recall vividly how God used Nehemiah to rebuild the walls of Jerusalem in just 52 days. Nehemiah did this through prayer and fasting, detailed preparation, showing his people how to work together and guiding them to fight the opposition. Those rebuilding the wall worked with a trowel in one hand and a sword in the other.

Nehemiah's story is a model of how any situation can be rebuilt for God's glory. This was true of Rose Hill Evangelical Free Church in South Dakota, which had gone through a difficult split. God healed the hurts and worked to restore this church. I was privileged to serve as Pastor during that time.

Many people today face broken marriages, serious job and economic issues, children who rebel and devastating illnesses. God can and does restore relationships, provide for His children, bring those in rebellion back to Himself and heal those who are ill. Not all such situations turn out "good" or the way we would like. But by faith we trust that God loves us and has our best interests in mind.

Nehemiah was interrupted by God when he volunteered to rebuild the walls of Jerusalem.

NEBUCHADNEZZAR

King Nebuchadnezzar was known for his vast building projects, such as the 400 foot high mountain terrace with flowing water and a hanging garden. This became one of the Seven Wonders of the World. But he was filled with pride. He said, "The king spoke, saying, 'Is not this great Babylon, that I have built for a royal dwelling by my mighty power and for the honor of my majesty?'" *Daniel 4:30*

God struck Nebuchadnezzar down because of his pride. Daniel chapter four and verse 33 tells of the king's fate, which went on for seven years.

"...He was driven away from people and ate grass like the ox. His body was drenched with the dew of heaven until his hair grew like the feathers of an eagle and his nails like the claws of a bird." *Daniel 4:33*

Nebuchadnezzar was interrupted by God because of his pride and he lived as an animal for seven years.

NEW TESTAMENT

JOSEPH

Joseph was a just man.

Imagine you are planning your wedding. It is to be one of the most wonderful occasions of your life. This is what Joseph was doing when he was interrupted by God.

Of all the characters in the narrative of the Nativity, perhaps the most overlooked person is Joseph. He was an honorable man who treated Mary with respect and dignity when it was found she was with child before they were married. He willingly endured public disgrace because he believed God's message from the angel that the child Mary was carrying was indeed The Son of God. He provided a fatherly influence for Jesus in terms of being a physically present, human father as Jesus was growing up. Joseph's life was not what he'd planned, but because he obeyed God, he was set apart to teach carpentry skills to the Savior of the world.

Joseph was interrupted by God when the angel appeared to him and his marriage plans were changed.

MARY

Mary, the Blessed Virgin, was the mother of Jesus, the Savior of the world.

Most biblical scholars agree that Mary was a young teenager pledged to be married to Joseph. But God interrupted those plans when the angel, Gabriel, appeared to her and declared that she would give birth to a Son, Jesus, Who would be "called the Son of the Most High" (Luke 1:32). The baby, Jesus, was conceived in her by God's Holy Spirit and was therefore fully God and fully man. Mary, who was obedient to God as she carried Jesus and raised Him in God's truth, was, however, a sinful human who needed her Son to save her, just as any other human needs salvation from sin. Her life was vastly different than she imagined it would be, but she was the nurturer of the Messiah, the Lord Jesus Christ. She knew great joy in her life because of this and will continue to be honored for her obedience to God's roadmap for her life.

Mary was interrupted by God when she was found to be with child when "...the power of the Most High..." overshadowed her.

STEPHEN

Stephen was the first martyr.

The Lord Jesus stood up when he viewed the stoning of Stephen from heaven (*Acts 7:56*). Stephen's life and death as a martyr influenced the Apostle Paul's life. When the stoning occurred, Paul was still known as Saul and had not yet been converted as a follower of Jesus Christ. No doubt the experience of witnessing the stoning of Stephen was instrumental in Saul's conversion.

The ending of Stephen's life was a very profound interruption. Stephen's brilliant testimony, which was a synopsis of a large part of the Old Testament, highlighting God's calling of Abraham, the freedom God gave the Israelites who were enslaved in Egypt, the ministry of Moses and the faithfulness of God's covenant promise to His people, so incensed the hypocritical religious leaders (Sanhedrin), that they violently stoned him to death. The testimony of Stephen, inspired by the Holy Spirit, convicted these religious leaders of their resistance to God's will and their part in the crucifixion of the Lord Jesus Christ. That is what drove them to kill Stephen.

Stephen was interrupted by God by being stoned by the Sanhedrin.

NICODEMUS

Nicodemus came to Jesus during the night.

Nicodemus, an important ruler of the Jews, was surprised when Jesus declared that Nicodemus needed to be born from above. The traditions Nicodemus had been taught were blown out of the water by the truth of God regarding sin and spiritual rebirth. Nicodemus apparently came to Christ.

"And Nicodemus, who at first came to Jesus by night, also came, bringing a mixture of myrrh and aloes, about a hundred pounds. Then they took the body of Jesus, and bound it in strips of linen with the spices, as the custom of the Jews is to bury." *John 19:39–40*

Nicodemus was interrupted by God during a late night visit with Jesus.

THE WOMAN AT THE WELL

Looking for love in all the wrong places.

This woman had committed adultery and was seeking to fill the void in her life through unhealthy relationships. She was performing the normal daily ritual of drawing drinking water from the town well, but she did so at a different time during the day so as not to be shunned by the "respectable" women. She was also a Samaritan, and Jews did not associated with Samaritans. It was during this time that the Lord Jesus, Who was resting by the well, showed respect and kindness to her by asking her for a drink of water and having a life–altering conversation with her.

The woman's life was forever changed when Jesus offered her the spiritual answer to her thirst for meaning. Instead of physical water, Jesus gave her salvation from sin and a relationship with God, which satisfied her every need: physical, spiritual, and intellectual. She was assured of eternal life in heaven because of this relationship to Jesus Christ as Savior.

The woman at the well was interrupted by God because of her thirst for Living Water.

ELIZABETH

"But they had no child, because Elizabeth was barren, and they were both well advanced in years." *Luke 1:7*

It's uncanny how the Lord works in barrenness (Sarah, Hanna and Rachel). Zacharias and Elizabeth were well advanced in age and had given up having a baby. It turns out that Elizabeth gives birth to John the Baptist.

Elizabeth was interrupted by God by giving birth to the great announcer of the Messiah.

About 21 other women are mentioned in the New Testament from Anna to Susanna, including Dorcas (Tabitha), Christian in Joppa converted under Paul's ministry to Lydia, converted under Paul's ministry in Philippi. All of them were interrupted by God in some way.

LUKE

Luke was a physician who may have served as a personal physician to the Apostle Paul.

Luke could have had a career as a successful physician in his time. **Colossians 4:14** confirms that Luke was a doctor. But his life was interrupted by God. Luke traveled with the Apostle Paul, participating in spreading the Gospel of Christ. Given the fact that many scholars believe Luke penned the Gospel of Luke and the book of Acts, it is possible that he, under the inspiration of the Holy Spirit, wrote 52 chapters of the New Testament.

Surely participating in telling the world of the cure to spiritual death (separation from God) as found in an encounter with the risen Lord Jesus far exceeds any achievements Luke would have had in terms of physical cures as a doctor.

Luke was interrupted by God through a drastic career change.

PAUL

Paul went from a life of persecuting Christians to proclaiming the Gospel to the world.

Originally named Saul of Tarsus until Jesus Christ changed his name to Paul, this Apostle had an impeccable religious pedigree as a Pharisee who was extremely well–versed in the Old Testament, including Mosaic Law.

As he was traveling to the town of Damascus with the purpose of persecuting Christians, the risen Lord Jesus Christ appeared to Saul. His dramatic conversion resulted in his three major missionary journeys where he proclaimed the Gospel to huge amounts of people. Paul endured extreme hardships, including torture and imprisonment. Paul was tireless in his telling the truth of the Gospel to everyone he encountered. He is credited as the author, inspired by the Holy Spirit, of nearly half of the New Testament.

Paul was interrupted by God because of a visit with Jesus face to face on the road to Damascus.

THE 12 APOSTLES

All of the Apostles were interrupted by God, including Peter (with his foot–shaped mouth), who, with his brother, Andrew, left their fishing careers. Matthew left his dishonest (yet lucrative) life as a tax collector, John was relieved of his fiery temper and the other men had their lives transformed when God interrupted their plans.

The 12 Apostles were interrupted by God by their willingness to become fishers of men.

2
CHRISTIAN LEADERS
PAST AND PRESENT

STOP

JOHN WESLEY (1703–1791)

John Wesley was an Anglican clergyman and evangelist who founded the Methodist Church with his brother, Charles.

Although I was raised in the Christian and Missionary Alliance Church in my hometown of Hawley, Minnesota, occasionally I would walk down the street to a small Methodist church. I remember listening to Reverend Hill, Reverend Nymark and Reverend Boyer preach. My father and I went to this church when there weren't services being held at our own.

John and his brother, Charles, were both methodic students of the Bible and founded the Methodist Church. Charles was a prolific hymn writer whose songs are still sung today.

John started out as a missionary to the New World. During a huge storm on the ship ride to America, he met a group of Moravian believers who had a unique spiritual peace that he was seeking.

His ministry to the Indian people living in the state of Georgia seemed to be a failure. Upon returning to England, he was deeply affected while reading Martin Luther's commentary on the book of Galatians. This text emphasized the scriptural doctrine of justification by grace through faith alone. Wesley later attended a service held by Moravian believers where Luther's commentary to the book of Romans was read aloud. It was not until that time that Wesley experienced conversion to faith in Christ.

John Wesley was interrupted by God while reading Martin Luther's commentary on the book of Romans.

GEORGE MUELLER (1805–1898)

George Mueller started out his life as a thief. He stole from his father and friends and ended up in prison with other thieves and murderers. After being released from prison, he took a long, hard look at his life.

Mueller enrolled in the University of Halle and also attended a Bible Study. Eventually he trusted Christ as his personal Savior.

Mueller began preaching and longed to be a missionary. He is known for his bold faith in God's provision. He and his wife trusted God alone for all they needed. He set the standard by asking God for his needs without telling anyone else about them. He started schools where he encouraged both children and adults to study the Bible. Mueller began five orphanages in England, where he kept more than 10,000 orphan children fed. Each child was provided for despite Mueller never asking anyone for money. He simply trusted God, who provided everything that was needed.

During his ministry he traveled 200,000 miles to 42 countries with the message, "And my God shall supply all your need according to His riches in glory by Christ Jesus." *Philippians 4:19*

George Mueller was interrupted by God while attending a Bible Study and accepted Christ as his Savior and supplier of his financial needs.

CHARLES FINNEY (1792–1875)

An American lawyer and president of Oberlin College, Charles Finney was a central figure in the religious movement of the 19th century. As the first professional evangelist, he was the originator of the "altar call."

Prior to knowing Christ, Finney abandoned his law career because he was required to study Mosaic Institutions (the Mosaic Law). This experience made him interested in the Bible, and upon careful study of it he converted to faith in Christ.

As he began to preach, he utilized the speaking techniques he learned as a lawyer. Specifically, his skill of pleading a case to a jury allowed him to effectively present the truth of the Gospel. God used Finney's skill in persuasive speech for His glory and many souls were saved.

Finney was part of the Presbyterian Church, but because he disagreed with some of their doctrines, he left and instead began preaching at the Broadway Tabernacle in 1834. He then became the minister at the Oberlin First Congregational Church and later served as president of Oberlin College from 1851–1866.

Charles Finney was interrupted by God when he earnestly studied the Scriptures.

CHARLES COLSON (1931–2012)

Charles "Chuck" Colson, who known as President Nixon's "hatchet man," was dramatically converted to Christ in 1973. He pled guilty to charges related to Watergate and entered prison in 1974.

After his experience in prison led him to begin a life–long ministry to those incarcerated. He founded Prison Fellowship in 1976 and influenced the church to truly begin a substantial ministry to prisoners.

The writer of several books, Colson penned "Born Again," which detailed the story of his conversion. He spoke to millions in person and had a far–reaching radio ministry. In addition, Colson had his hand on the pulse of American culture and politics. He is known for his insightful commentaries regarding these.

He founded The Chuck Colson Center for Christian Worldview in 2009 as a training and research facility. The work of Prison Fellowship reaches over 100 countries.

Charles Colson was interrupted by God when he came to know Christ after the Watergate Scandal, in his car.

JOSH McDOWELL (BORN 1936)

Josh McDowell, a Christian apologist, writer and evangelist, was born in Union City, Michigan. One of five children, he struggled with low self–esteem and had a father who was an alcoholic and abusive. McDowell was sexually abused as a child from age six to thirteen.

When he began college, he decided to become an agnostic. He researched and started to write a paper to disprove the Christian faith. While working on this paper, he was convinced that the Bible and its claims were true and embraced Christ as his Savior.

He earned a Master of Divinity degree. His most well–known books are "More than a Carpenter" and "Evidence that Demands a Verdict." His humility is to be noted as well as his intellect.

Josh McDowell was interrupted by God when he set out to disprove Christianity and decided to embrace it.

RAVI ZACHARIAS (BORN 1946) – Christian Apologist

At age 17, Ravi attempted suicide by swallowing poison. In the hospital his mother read to him John 14 and in particular John 14:19, "Because I live, you also will live." Ravi said "Please get me out of the hospital and I promise I will leave no stone unturned in my pursuit of truth."

Born in India he moved to Canada and eventually to the United States. Charles Colson called him the greatest apologist of our time. He is a world traveler, speaking to Universities, college campuses, seminaries, etc. He is a best-selling author and has a daily radio program "Just Thinking."

Ravi Zacharias was interrupted by God when his mother read to him John 14:7 while recovering from an attempted suicide.

C. S. LEWIS (1898–1963)

Clive Staples Lewis was an atheist whose life was interrupted when God impressed His truth upon this writer's mind and heart. Although raised in a Christian family, he embraced atheism. Later, after much study and discussion with J. R. R. Tolkien and G. K. Chesterton, Lewes reconverted to Christianity. He noted, "I came into Christianity kicking and screaming."

This prolific writer, who was born in Ireland, yet resided in England, penned 58 books, including scholarly works, fiction, science fiction and apologetics. He developed and excellent argument to defend Christ's claim to be the Son of God. A concise picture of what has been called "Lewis' trilemma."

Assuming that the Gospels are accurate, Lewis said there are three options:

Jesus was telling falsehoods and knew it, and so He was a liar.

Jesus was telling falsehoods but believed He was telling the truth and so He was insane.

Jesus was telling the truth, and so He was divine.

The life of C. S. Lewis included tragedy as he was injured in World War I and endured the struggle and eventual death of his wife, Joy, due to cancer. His mother died when he was a young boy.

C. S. Lewis wrote many top selling books. He is much quoted in the 21st century.

C. S. Lewis was interrupted by God when God impressed His truth upon this writer's mind and heart.

FANNY CROSBY

If you have attended a church where hymns are sung as part of the worship, then you probably sang a few of the 13,000 hymn lyrics written by Fanny Crosby. As a child, her doctor made a grave error with her medication and she lost her sight. Truly her life as she imagined it was interrupted by God. However, in His infinite wisdom, God gifted Fanny Crosby with the ability to compose theologically correct, poetic, inspired texts that were set to music by various musicians. Some of her better known titles are: **Blessed Assurance, To God Be the Glory, Safe in the Arms Of Jesus**.

Fanny Crosby's writing was so prolific that she used a pseudonym for some of her texts. While we cannot know (this side of heaven) what God's specific purposes for suffering are, it is reasonable to believe that Fanny Crosby might not have written so much had she not lost her sight as a young girl. We know that myriads of people have been encouraged in their walk with Christ by these hymns and that countless numbers of people have come to know Christ through these songs of truth and praise. It has been said that wisdom is "looking at life from God's perspective." Wisdom sees the purpose God had in the interruption He allowed to occur in Fanny Crosby's life.

Fanny Crosby was interrupted by God by blindness.

CORRIE TEN BOOM

As part of a Christian family in the Netherlands, Corrie ten Boom provided safe haven for many Jewish individuals when the Nazi regime was raging. Amazingly, the families and individuals who hid in the large ten Boom home in Holland remained safe and escaped into freedom. Corrie's family, tragically, was arrested and sent to various concentration camps. Despite the intense suffering she and her sister, Betsie, endured, they grew closer to Christ in the midst of the cruelty of the prison guards. To describe becoming a captive in a concentration camp an interruption does not seem adequate. But the way in which God worked in their lives and used them for His glory is tremendous.

Corrie and Betsie were able to keep a small Bible with them in their bunks. The spaces they stayed in became infested with fleas. Because the camp guards wanted to avoid the fleas, Corrie and Betsie were able to have Bible studies with the some of the others in their barracks. Corrie and Betsie counted it joy to have the fleas so that they could have unhindered time to study the Bible. If you were in that situation, how would you react?

This story does have a positive ending. Although her father and her sister died in prison, Corrie was released due to a "clerical error." Clearly her release was orchestrated by God. After her release, Corrie ministered to many survivors of the camps and other war atrocities. She traveled frequently and spoke to many about her horrific experiences and how God changed her and used her life for His glory.

The book she wrote about her experience, The Hiding Place, was mad into a major motion picture. Countless people have been impacted by her story and how she learned that God is good, faithful, trustworthy and wise despite terrible circumstances and unimaginable suffering. Her testimony of God's healing in her life has inspired thousands of people. According to the Holocaust Encyclopedia, for her dedicated assistance to the Jews, she received the distinction of being one of the "Righteous Among the Nations" in December of 1967, by the Yad Vashem Remembrance Authority.

Corrie ten Boom was interrupted by God by persecution in the Holocaust.

JONI EARECKSON TADA

In 1967, at the age of 17, Joni Eareckson Tada experienced a devastating diving accident which left her in a quadriplegic state. Despite this situation, which includes a minimal use of her hands, Joni completed two years of rehabilitation and re–joined her family and began pursuing work as an artist using her mouth to hold the paintbrush. She continued to love and serve Jesus as an author, speaker, recording artist and a champion of individuals with disabilities. Her ministry, Joni and Friends International Disability Center began in 1979 at her home and has blossomed into a wonderful organization affecting and blessing the lives of millions.

Joni Eareckson Tada is married to Ken Tada and has experienced an amazing life of change in her inner self as well as the well as the truly difficult disability that has changed her earthly body. Yet her acceptance of what occurred, and her trust in God despite all her trials is an inspiration to countless people around the world. She is a shining light for the truth of the Gospel of Jesus Christ and the hope found only in Him. She continually points to heaven, where her body will not be bound by quadriplegia and she will be free of physical pain. But her higher calling is to bring others to a knowledge of Jesus and to look forward to meeting Jesus face to face.

Joni Eareckson Tada was interrupted by God because of a diving accident.

CHAPTER 3

TESTIMONIES BY
FAMILY AND FRIENDS

Each of us have people close to us who have experienced drastic, life–changing interruptions. The following accounts are from some of my family and friends that have impacted me significantly. **They have all been interrupted by God**.

In September of 1993, I became the Pastor of Audubon Chapel in Audubon, MN. Audubon is about 7 miles west of Detroit Lakes, MN. One of the members was the Weinert Family. They had four children in their family: three girls and one boy. The middle girl, Kim, was interrupted by God by a tragic death in her family.

Testimony of Kim Weinert Erickson

July 4, 2004 will forever be etched in my memory. The story God was writing with my life took a curve I never saw coming and would never have chosen. God has a way of doing that in His incredible sovereignty. That fact is what makes me so thankful He is the one writing the story and working out all the details of my life for His glory and my ultimate good.

My husband and I had two beautiful little boys, Caleb, who was 21 months old and Micah, who was 4 months old. I loved my life just the way it was. I had a wonderful husband and I had always wanted to raise boys and was doing so. We were celebrating the Fourth of July holiday with his family and had a busy day filled with a community church service, a big lunch at our house, some fun at my in–laws' farm, and we were wrapping up with a big fireworks show. The fireworks show was being held in a nearby small town. We all traveled there in several vehicles and were in a hurry to get a good seat as thousands of people attend this event.

When we arrived, I remember the scene was quite chaotic. There were cars parking everywhere, people all over the place, and it was dusk. After parking, everyone in our van hopped out immediately except my husband. I took Micah and placed him in his car seat on the grass while I went to set up the stroller where I would place the car seat.

While my back was turned setting it up, my husband was told he had to move our van. We all told him he was clear to move it and he immediately began to back up. <u>After a few feet, he put it in drive and ended up placing the front, right, passenger wheel on top of Micah in his car seat. From that moment on, our lives changed forever.</u>

We were actually just yards away from a hospital. Someone scooped up the car seat and we ran him directly into the trauma room. The staff worked fiercely to stabilize him and after some time had gone by, informed us he would have to be air lifted to the next larger town but there would be no room for either one of us in the helicopter. A friend raced my husband the 90 miles to that town to beat the helicopter there so papers could be signed, while I stayed with Micah until they could stabilize him enough to place him in the helicopter.

My in–laws drove me to the next hospital <u>and it was the longest drive of my life</u>. However, God met me in that car that night. I began to have this conversation with God in my head. I was pleading with him to spare my son. At that time, there was a song that used to be on the radio quite often. The song talked about how sometimes God calms the storm, and other time He chooses to calm His child. I began telling God that I needed Him to calm the storm and it was as if I could hear Him say to me, "No, this time, I am going to calm you." I went back and forth with God, begging Him to calm the storm and feeling Him impress on my heart that He was going to calm me and the storm was going to rage. Psalm 23 and the line from it, "Even though I walk through the valley of the shadow of death, I will fear no evil..." also kept running through my mind. I would tell God I didn't want to go through that valley and I felt Him assure me we were headed there but He would comfort me and walk through it with me.

By the time I reached the hospital, I felt God had prepared my heart that Micah would not be alive when I got there. <u>He was not. I found my husband in a side room off the emergency room, rocking our lifeless son</u>. The doctors had come to him earlier and said there was nothing more they could do and my husband held our son as he died. We were catapulted into journey we never saw coming, and I am so thankful we did not because we never would have chosen this path. We would have missed all the things God had to teach us about who He is and all that He would do as a result of that little life.

Those events took place over 11 years ago and God has been teaching us about His sovereignty, His sufficient grace and His hope ever since. God began to change me and my husband that day. I could fill a book with the way He changed us, the things He taught us, the lives we saw changed, and the incredible things God did as a result of this tragedy He wrote into our story. One of the greatest things I learned was though I would never have written this chapter into my story, God knows best and I wouldn't want to give up who I discovered God to be as a result of those dark waters I had to wade through. Isaiah 43 tells us we will pass through water and we will walk through fires, it is not if but when. The passage also says God will be with us during those times and He is, and without those difficult times, we cannot know God in the same way.

It was during those hard months and even years after our accident that I discovered a deep and satisfying joy in simply knowing God intimately. Real joy is found in just knowing Him, not in anything we have of do. 1 Peter 1:8–9 says "rejoice with inexpressible and glorious joy, because you are receiving the goal of your faith, the salvation of your souls." It is that inexpressible joy that I discovered even in the darkest of days. Every day for many months I read Lamentations 3:19–26. In those verses it says that the Lord is our portion. It means He is the goal, the inheritance. Just knowing Him and getting to be with Him is what makes the salvation of our souls so wonderful! Because of all we have in store for us, we have a hope and these are the thoughts that got me through my days.

Since that summer of 2004, God has richly blessed us. I had always said I wanted a bunch of boys and twins (boys or girls). Sometimes God shows us the sweetest grace in granting the silly desires of our hearts. He gave us two more boys, and then twin girls. Today our children are ages 12, 9, 7, 6 and 6. God's hand has clearly been at work in and through this tragedy of losing our son. I will close with telling you one of the ways God confirmed to us that He was at work and had not forgotten us or made a mistake.

Two months after our accident, we discovered we were expecting another baby. We began to discuss names and the name Noah came up. For some reason, when Micah was on the way we had said we liked the name Noah, but we would save it for a third boy if we ever had one and would name our second son Micah. So, when we discovered a third child was on the way after Micah was gone, we said if it was a boy, we should name him Noah as that is what we had decided earlier. We looked up what the name Noah meant, and God put His sovereignty on display before us. Noah's name means "provider of comfort." God is good and working all thing for His glory and our good which is to make us more like His Son (Romans 8:28–29) no matter what difficult chapters He may bring into our lives.

The Erickson Family

Kim and her husband Todd were interrupted by God by the death of their son, Micah.

Todd is the Child Evangelism Fellowship Director of North Dakota Inc Northeast Chapter.

KIM McCONACHIE

I was born in Houston, TX, on February 23, 1976. My family moved to The Woodlands, TX, in 1982 and I consider that my home.

My family was Catholic, and we did all the proper Catholic traditions. Religion, however, was not a guiding force in my life. Many summers I went to Bible camp with one of my friends. Our family said our dinner and bedtime prayers. But it was just something we did, not something we lived. My mother was diagnosed with breast cancer in 1992 and when our priest was not compassionate regarding my mother's health, my family discontinued association with the Catholic church. We still continued with our prayers, and I know my family still believed in God.

My main activity in school was sports, which I loved. I started playing soccer in grade school and played until I graduated from high school. My Dad was my coach for many years. I was also on the track team in high school.

We had a good family life. I graduated from high school in 1994 and when my parents and younger sister moved to Nebraska in January 1995, I stayed in The Woodlands because I considered it my home.

On October 14, 1995, my life changed forever. As we did each week, my friends and I were out riding ATV's (All Terrain Vehicles). But this day proved to be different. I was involved in a serious accident and experienced a stroke, a Traumatic Brain Injury (TBI) and a broken neck.

During the week after my accident, I underwent several brain surgeries to relieve pressure on my brain and remove injured brain tissue. I was placed in a medically induced coma. **On October 20, 1995, my body began to shut down and the decision was made to remove me from life support.** Miraculously, just hours before the life support was to be disconnected, my organs began to function on their own. I was truly a medical miracle, because within days I was completely removed from life support.

I remember that the doctor said to me once I was awake, "We do not know if you will ever be able to talk or walk again or be able to tell the difference between sweet and sour." Even though I couldn't talk at that point, I remember thinking, "Well, why in the world did you wake me up?"

As my family and the medical staff would later see, God had a specific plan for me after my life was interrupted by the accident and injuries. God shattered the notion that I would not talk or walk.

Even after being released from the hospital, I continued my therapy on an outpatient basis. I was not excited about this at all. Therapy included re–learning to walk with assistance, performing leg lifts and numerous hours of occupational therapy to try and regain the use of my left arm. Though this process was grueling, I knew I didn't have a choice but to do it. With the help and support of my family, I made it successfully through therapy.

I am certain that without this interruption in my life that God allowed, I would not have come to know Jesus Christ as my Lord and Savior. Growing up, my family and I attended church each week, but I did not know Christ personally. In 1995, I moved to Omaha, NE to be with my parents and continue to adjust to living with my limitations.

My neighbor invited me to church and I was so affected by Christ's truth that I went to church at every opportunity. I began serving with a street evangelism ministry in Omaha's inner–city. During this time, I met Brian McConachie, a fellow believer. We fell in love and were married in the fall of 2008. I am convinced that Brian and I would not have met if my accident had not occurred. Having him as my husband and friend is s tremendous blessing that God showered upon me, despite the truly difficult circumstances of my accident.

Brian and I enjoy working on our home, spending time with family and friends and watching movies. I enjoy times with my nephews and honorary nieces and my time at work. I'm employed by the before and after school care program at a local elementary school. In addition, I make regular trips to Texas to participate in fishing and trap shooting.

I can testify to the truth of God's perfect sovereign plan for my life and for all of our lives. He has given me a wonderful life filled with countless blessings. Because of His love and joy that flows in my life daily, I can say to each person I meet, "God bless you!

Kim was interrupted by God when an ATV accident interrupted her life.

JOY BARRINGER

(written by Naomi Barringer, my daughter)

Naomi gave a speech at a women's conference after the birth of Joy. The following are the notes for her talk.

Blessings

Performed by *Laura Story*
Written by *Laura Mixon Story, Liz Story*

We pray for blessings
We pray for peace
Comfort for family, protection while we sleep
We pray for healing, for prosperity
We pray for Your mighty hand to ease our suffering
All the while, You hear each spoken need
Yet love us way too much to give us lesser things

'Cause what if Your blessings come through raindrops
What if Your healing comes through tears
What if a thousand sleepless nights
Are what it takes to know You're near
What if trials of this life are Your mercies in disguise

We pray for wisdom
Your voice to hear
And we cry in anger when we cannot feel You near
We doubt Your goodness, we doubt Your love
As if every promise from Your Word is not enough
All the while, You hear each desperate plea
And long that we'd have faith to believe

'Cause what if Your blessings come through raindrops
What if Your healing comes through tears
What if a thousand sleepless nights
Are what it takes to know You're near
And what if trials of this life are Your mercies in disguise
When friends betray us
When darkness seems to win
We know that pain reminds this heart
That this is not, this is not our home
It's not our home

'Cause what if Your blessings come through raindrops
What if Your healing comes through tears
And what if a thousand sleepless nights
Are what it takes to know You're near
What if my greatest disappointments
Or the aching of this life
Is the revealing of a greater thirst this world can't satisfy

And what if trials of this life
The rain, the storms, the hardest nights
Are Your mercies in disguise

I sang that song at church 5 weeks before Joy was born–little did I know that it would take on a completely different meaning.

Jim was done having children after 2 boys. I was not. God changed Jim's mind and little Jacob was born. He apologized to me for a long time after that because he couldn't imagine life without his "spicy meatball" as Jim likes to call him. But this time he was definitely done. But imagine his surprise when I texted him a picture of the pregnancy test and it was even more of a surprise when the ultrasound tech. said, "it's a girl!"

Joy arrived on Wednesday, June 1, 2011 after a long day of back labor with no drugs.

After a few hours she started having respiratory distress. After being in the level 2 nursery it was determined that they needed help and they said that a team was coming to pick her up. Devastation overtook me. What was going on?? I felt hot all over and they sat me down for fear that I would faint. As we walked down the hallway of the NICU there were baby pictures that lined the hallways. They were all hooked up to tubes and were hard to look at. I was trying to be strong. We rounded the corner only to learn that we had beat the ambulance there. My heart sunk. Something was wrong. They sat us down in the hallway waiting area and we waited. Sick to our stomachs with worry and confusion. Why was this happening??

The elevator doors opened and there they were, three people wheeled her right past us while the fourth one stopped. She said that she had trouble with Joy's oxygen levels and had to intubate her (we would later learn that she had a pulmonary hemorrhage, but she didn't share that info at the time).

We finally got into the room and we were immediately inundated with papers and information. We were told that we could stay in her room with her on the futon because there were no rooms available in the Ronald McDonald house.

It was now 2:00am and we tried to lay down but we were restless and both felt nauseous.

Every family in the NICU has a social worker and she came to see us in the early morning hours of Thursday. She took care of getting us a room at the Ronald McDonald house (which is on the same floor as the NICU in the hospital). She arranged for a breast pump for me to start pumping and parking passes. Oh my goodness, such a blessing it was to have someone to take care of us in our confusion and weariness.

Thursday was the worst day of my life to date. I was a roller coaster of emotions as things spiraled out of control. They kept having to up her ventilator until they couldn't turn it up anymore and then she had a pnumo thorax which is a hole in the lung with air escaping and then pushing on the lung. The other lung was collapsed and they had to put in a chest tube. It all came to a head when we were in her room and the nurse said very calmly "I'm going to press this button and there will be a lot of people running in here." It took me a minute to realize that she was calling a code blue on our baby Joy.

We were asked to wait in the hallway which seemed to be spinning now and my face was burning from the tears. I felt as though my stomach might actually explode.

Earlier in the day they had told us that it was a possibility that she had PPHN but not to Google it because it would scare us and she probably didn't have it. Now they came out into the hallway and told us that she did have it and that there was nothing else that they could do except put her in this machine that would keep her alive while her lungs healed.

Our heads were spinning as she tried to explain in dumbed down terms what would happen. She looked at us as if she knew we really didn't understand and said, "If we don't do this, she won't make it."

Weeping does not adequately explain what we did and how we felt.

She said we could come and see her before the surgery. Up until that point the nurses had been telling us not to touch her because they didn't want her to be overstimulated. But now they said to touch her and that we could pray with her. I really felt that they were telling us to say goodbye.

How does one adequately convey enough love for a lifetime in one minute? We cried and my tears were literally falling on her. Jim prayed and we tried to hug her and then they whisked her away.

We were left with the doctor that needed the consent form signed and she went over the awful risks, brain bleeds, seizures, brain damage, hearing loss and often death. What could we do? We signed. It was up to God now.

We somberly walked down the hallway to the Ronald McDonald house and all of a sudden there were ten family members and friends that arrived within minutes of each other, right when we needed them the most. We formed a circle and prayed. We found out that our church at that moment was having a prayer vigil for baby Joy and we were in awe of God's prompting and timing.

As we were praying, tears flooded my face as God's presence filled my soul. In the middle of praying the nurse said that the doctor wanted to see us.

That was the longest, most somber walk down three hallways. It was like a horrible scene from a movie. Walking hand in hand down the last hallway, which now seemed like a mile long, we could see the doctor waiting at the end and I immediately started to assess his mood and what news he had for us. As we approached he said, "That went great!" Relief!

He said we could see her in a bit. We sat down to breathe a little sigh of relief, but when we went back to see her it was a horrible nightmarish sight. She was really puffy, she had two cannulas coming out of her neck with blood flowing through them, machines and tubes everywhere. I could barely keep from falling to my knees. What was happening to my sweet baby girl?

They told us she could be on the ECMO machine for days or weeks.

"Breathe in Jesus, breathe out Jesus" is all I could do to get through.

Jesus had to have been literally holding me up. He was in that room with us in such a real and powerful way.

The nurses made us go to our room at the Ronald McDonald House down the hallway. We were numb as we laid in the bed trying to get sleep to come. We cried, prayed and pleaded with God.

I couldn't help but think that I would soon be planning my baby girl's funeral. What would I do with all of the clothes and the crib? I would not be able to go into her room when we got home.

I was finally able to take a shower in the early hours of Friday morning, the first since giving birth! I had not cared at all. As I stood in that shower the phrase "the dark night of the soul" came to mind. I remember my dad saying that was how he felt after suffering his stroke. I didn't know what it meant until that moment.

I cried out to God to hold my baby girl and to help me to not lose heart or my trust and praise to Him.

I met God in a new way in that shower. Out of desperation He revealed a new part of His sustaining and faithful power that I will never fully be able to explain or understand.

Our nights were filled with pumping, praying, reading Scripture and then walking down the three hallways to her room to deliver the milk. All the while, the song blessings going through my head. **"What if a thousand sleepless nights are what it takes to know You're near?"**

I felt Him. I REALLY felt Him.

Once in her room, we would visit with the nurse and find out her numbers and the results of any x–rays and labs. We would pray over her, sing and then return to the room to try and rest for an hour or so. Then we would wake up to do it again.

I will admit that there were a few times I wondered if the nurses thought I was crazy for pumping. I thought maybe they were thinking to themselves "this baby will never survive to need that milk." But I did it every two hours. My prayer was to nurse this baby.

Our days were spent visiting her in her room where I would sing to her. The first full day that she was on ECMO I pulled up a chair next to her and started to sing. I would barely get a few words out and then breakdown weeping over her. My voice was shaky but Father God was sustaining me with new songs to sing. The words to old familiar songs had new meaning and were sung as prayers and praise to God in a way I had never sung before. The Holy Spirit power in that room was so very strong. I on my own would never have been able to handle it.

There were several different nurses over the course of our stay but all agreed that when I sang, her stats were more favorable. God was ministering to me by bringing songs to mind and I was ministering to her.

If you would have told me a week before she was born that we would go through this I would say that I would never have been able to make it through, but something beautiful happens when you are at the end of yourself.

Growing up I heard that "God will never give you more than you can handle," but He does, He does so that you can be desperate for Him. His strength is made perfect in our weakness. We were completely and utterly desperate for Him. God's Word came alive in a new way and I couldn't get enough of it. It was literally holding us up.

Jim and I had a church service in the chapel on the Sunday morning after ECMO and it was one of the most intimate and spiritually meaningful times that we have ever experienced. We just started praising God and we both started singing "Our God is greater, our God is stronger, God You are higher than any other, Our God is Healer, Awesome in power, our God, our God."

We read scripture and God's powerful Word washed over our souls and brought such comfort and supernatural peace. It was beautiful.

My outlet was singing to her and on occasion Jim sang with me. But his outlet was the Caring Bridge site. He told me that if they told him to stand on his head in her room that it would help he would, but he felt helpless. He realized that he had an audience and he told me he was going for it with the gospel. Otherwise what was this all for? It would be for nothing!

The outpouring of God's provision through His people was nothing short of amazing.

People taking our boys to help my mom, visitors at just the right time to pray with us, texts and messages filled with God's Word, just the right verse to get us through, the amazing people at the hospital, a doctor who is a believer, nurses who lovingly cared for Joy and for us and a woman named Dianne who is a child psychologist. She helped us when the boys came to visit. They visited twice, once when things were pretty grim, boy, did God use her to meet with them and answer their questions and to prepare them for what they would see. God protected their little hearts that day, but obviously they realized the severity.

The next day Josiah asked my mom if he could stay home from school and fast and pray.

Jesse kept saying "I'm just not praying enough" which is ironic, because no one in our family prays as much as that kid. He prayed every day for Joy while I was pregnant and would end his prayer with "and let her do great things for You, God."

God was already using her, using her life or her homegoing to bring glory to Himself and to get people praying and seeking.

What a faith builder this was for the boys. Not what we would have chosen, but God's ways are not our ways and His thoughts are not our thoughts.

Joy, to the shock and amazement of her doctors and nurses was able to slowly but surely be able to be weaned off ECMO after only five days. The nurses kept saying that they couldn't believe it. It was the power of believers crying out to God in prayer. I like to think of God going, "Ok, ok, enough already! Talk about praying without ceasing!"

God kept surprising all of the medical staff with her strides to recovery. Each nurse would stop in to visit and see how well she was doing and wouldn't be able to stop commenting about how this never happens.

The Holy Spirit helped us to quickly point out that it was The Great Physician who had done the work. Looking back on this whole situation I think about all of the people that God brought to us that He was able to speak to through us.

Some beautiful ladies visited and brought me stacks of blank cards. I was prompted to write each of the nurses a card at the end of their shifts and include the gospel in it. That wasn't me, it was HIM. I was able to share with them the Hope and Joy that only Jesus can bring.

One dear lady I had the honor to meet was another Dianne. She was the cleaning lady for the NICU. I saw her nearly every day. She told me at the end of our stay that she had purposely lingered while cleaning and mopping by our room so she could hear me sing. She said it was an angel in that room.

I laughed thinking about how awful it must have sounded through the tears, but honored that I got to share the joy of song that the Holy Spirit gave me. I got to talk for almost 45 minutes with her about God's love and the miracle He had done.

And then there was Marie, the nurse who worked the night shift several times. One of the nights was the one year anniversary of her father's death and we talked most of the night about having a relationship with Jesus Christ.

There were countless other encounters, some big, some seemingly small, but all divinely orchestrated by our Awesome God.

I don't tell you any of this to brag about Jim or myself but to brag and attest to the miraculous work of the Holy Spirit to give joy despite circumstance.

We had the name Joy picked out years ago in case Jesse was a girl, but only God knew what her name would really come to mean to us and those around us who were touched by His story through her.

Joy is something you experience totally outside of circumstances. Circumstances cause us to look at arrival points or destinations. Looking forward to the next big thing or event. Can't stand your job? Think about the weekend. Although weekends offer some satisfaction and pleasure, the feeling is not sustainable. The reason people have joy is because of their being in God's presence day after day. They have a deep emotional understanding of their dependence on God. When we spend time with Him, we know Him, we know His character. We trust Him and what His Word says. We trust that He is faithful.

May God bless you with eyes to see what lessons might be learned through trials and may He give you His unexplainable joy despite circumstances because He is faithful.

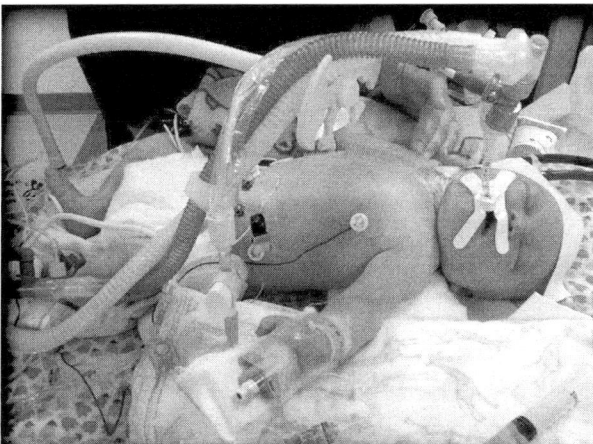

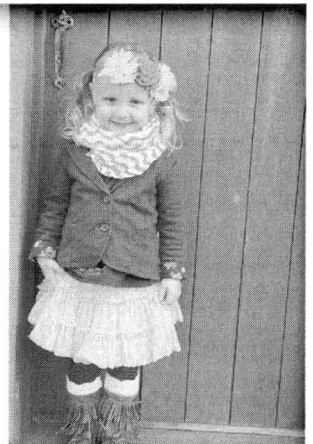

Jim and Naomi were interrupted by God through the birth of Joy.

HERB SIEMENS

Herb Siemens lives in Fargo, North Dakota with Anni his wife of 41 years. He is an elder at Calvary Church at Village Green where they attend. He grew up being a Mennonite. Herb is Senior Vice President – Global & Strategic Planning at Fargo Assembly Company which has seventeen plants in seven states plus one in England.

The summer of 1968 was going well. We lived on a small mixed farm that was never able to pay all the bills but we always had enough to live on and the rest didn't matter, at least not to me. I had just turned 17, and was enjoying an easygoing summer of working on the farm and a few odd jobs for some neighbors. I did not have a lot of cares or concerns in my life.

Then on July 31 at around 7:30 PM, my life got interrupted by God big time. My oldest sister Linda and her fiancé Pete came out from the city (Winnipeg) to have supper with the family as they did on most Wednesday nights. It was a beautiful summer evening, great to be outside. After supper Pete, my brother Ken and I took our old pickup (I was driving) and went out in the fields chasing foxes. We each had a loaded shotgun in the cab of the truck with us. The loaded guns in the cab were illegal, but we were just young guys having fun on some back roads and didn't pay attention to those details.

It didn't take long till we saw a fox and gave chase. When it stopped at the side of the road, I skidded to a stop and we all jumped out of the pickup. That is when my life was interrupted. My loaded twelve gauge gun was under the seat, when I hurriedly pulled it out from under the seat the hammer hooked on the seat bottom and the gun went off. It hit me in mid–thigh in my right leg from about 12–18 inches away. Six inches lower and it would have blown out my knee.

I almost died several different times that night. In all the panic, I almost bled to death before they remembered to put a tourniquet on my leg. When Pete drove us back to the farm after the accident we came within inches of rolling the pickup, which would have turned out very badly. God was surely with me that evening.

My parents drove me to the hospital in our family car (with a police escort). I remember lying on the backseat during the drive, my Mother asked my dad what they had done that was so bad that the family had to be punished like this. I also remember her asking my dad if he thought I would have to stay in the hospital overnight. The reality of how serious this was had not yet set in.

The first three surgeons who looked at my leg when we got to the ER and all of them said there was no hope, they had to amputate the leg. They went and asked another surgeon who was operating on a car accident victim; he looked at my leg and said he thought he could save it. This was a young surgeon named Reginald Wightman who we found out later was considered a bit of a rebel among the other surgeons. So after he finished operating on the car accident victim it was my turn (by now it was the middle of the night). The next morning he came on rounds accompanied by the chief surgeon and they checked out my leg. The chief surgeon chastised my doctor and said that he had made a big mistake with the surgery. He should have amputated my leg, because there was no doubt that I would be back in less than a year and they would have to take the leg anyway.

Looking at the situation, I was a real mess. There was a four inch hole in my thigh that went all the way down around the bone, number six buckshot can make a real mess. It had severed the artery, the veins, the nerves and a whole lot of muscle. It turns out the biggest problem with all of this over the years was the nerve damage, in 1968 they had not yet invented reconstructive nerve surgery. The blood circulation problems have also presented a lot of challenges. Five months later at Christmas, the wound had still not grown completely shut. I had to change the dressing every day to keep it clean. It was February before it was finally closed.

I did end up spending 100 days in the hospital. I spent a couple weeks in ICU, then five weeks on the ward. After that I was transferred to a rehab hospital for seven weeks to learn how to walk again. Spending that much time inside was very difficult for a young farm kid. It was well over a month before I was actually allowed to sit up. By October I was finally allowed some day passes; first to get out just for the day and eventually I could even stay at home over Saturday night.

The chief surgeon was proved wrong. It is 46 plus years later and I still have my leg, or at least most of it. The circulation problems and nerve damage were so bad that it didn't take long before we had to amputate the toes, some just the end and some the whole toe. For many years, I battled with chronic infection in my leg.

Over the years I had a lot of different problems with my leg and as a result I spent years walking on crutches. Life does move on, I got married and we had four children. When the kids were small and played, one of them (whoever was the dad) always pretended to be on crutches because for them it was so normal.

I have to wear a surgical compression stocking (unless I am lying down) to force the blood back up my leg. Because of the nerve damage I have very poor, almost no sensation in most of my leg. It is worst in my foot, but it does go all the way up and over my knee. I wear a custom made insole to spread out the pressure points on the bottom of my foot. Over the years my ankle has fused itself, so that really complicates walking and just keeping my balance. It is weird, but one of the things I miss the most is not being able to feel the grass under my foot.

On the flip side of what I have said so far, my life is great. I feel truly blessed by God in every way. We are supposed to be thankful for all things and in all circumstances. I confess that I have not always been thankful along the way, but I can truly say that today I am very happy with my "Lot in Life." I have a great wife Anni who has been extremely supportive for over 41 years of marriage. Without her help, I don't think I could have managed it. We had four children who are all married to terrific spouses. We have eleven beautiful Grandchildren who keep us quite active. God has truly blessed us.

My leg is in better shape now than it has been for 46 years. Three years ago, just before I turned 60 I walked a half marathon. For a guy who for years had trouble walking around the block, I couldn't believe that something like that was possible. I doubt I will ever try that again but being able to do it once was really neat.

My life got interrupted back in 1968, but by the truly amazing grace of God I can say that I am truly Thankful to Him for everything he has brought my way.

Herb was interrupted by God via a twelve gauge shotgun.

GEORGE FINCKE

(a bishop in the Episcopal Church)

My friend, Dr. George Fincke, a fellow stroke–overcomer, wrote the following:

"I had a stroke ('a bleed'–a hemorrhagic stroke – only about 17% of all strokes are this kind) on October 12, 2000. It took two months in a hospital and a rehab facility, and about a year to learn how to walk and talk again. My right side is still affected, though not paralyzed, and 'they' tell me that means my stroke was in the left hemisphere of my brain. I walk slowly, and with a bit of a limp. One thing that does remain is called aphasia, where there is a difficulty moving my thoughts from my brain to my mouth, at times, there is a disconnect of frustrating proportion. I know what I want to say, but...

I am convinced I 'sang myself' to where I am today, by the grace of God. I started with children's songs ('I've Been Workin on the Railroad' is a favorite). I am a PK, a preacher's kid, so hymns have factored large in my life. A dear friend brought me a CD called "The Hymn Collection" by the Huddersfield Choral Society, and I forced myself to sing with the glorious choir for an hour every day. The Bible talks about the power of music. Think of shepherd David ministering music to a troubled King Saul or Paul telling us to sing and make melody in our hearts unto the Lord. It is a true spiritual therapy."

Bishop Fincke was interrupted by God with a stroke.

KENNETH QUAM

I don't remember Kenny. I was barely 2 years old when he died. I remember folks talking about him, about his tremendous strength, his athletic skill and his scholarly aptitude.

The following was written by my brother, Butch:

"In the fall of 1944, a young man by the name of Kenneth Ralph Quam was injured in the head while playing football in Hawley, MN. Unknown to him and others he had developed a brain tumor. Painful headaches followed for weeks. In October he had surgery in Rochester, MN. His father Andrew and his mother Louise accompanied him to the Mayo Clinic. His father's last words to his son before the operation were, "Give your heart to Christ, Kenny," to which his son replied, "All right Dad." After the surgery, his father left for home to work and to pray with their church. The church was having special meetings with Rev. Abe Voth at the time. Kenny's mother stayed with her son after the surgery. Later she prayed alone into the night for him. About 4:00am, she finally gave her son over to the Lord, praying, "I give him to you. Let him die; only save his soul." At 7:00am that morning, Kenny passed away. Three months after a large and sad funeral, a cousin of Kenny had a dream. The dream was later revealed to Kenny's father Andrew Quam. In the dream the cousin saw Kenny, who told her, "Tell Mom I'm saved."

The following are the lyrics to a song written by me – Kenny's younger brother (David Quam). The song is a prayer from heaven by Kenny. The music is from the opera "The Pearl Fischers" by Georges Bizet.

A few fleeting years
Filled with laughter and tears;
His Mama prayed all night;
His Daddy urged him on to the light.
Tell my Mother,
Tell her that I'm saved.
Tell my Father,
Streets up here with gold are paved.
I have been redeemed,
Bought with the blood and am now set free.
I am born again;
Some day you will all come join me.
I saw my sinful condition;
I saw Christ, my redemption,
And now I've received my salvation.
So tell my Mother,
Tell her that I'm saved.
Tell my Father,
Streets up here with gold are paved.
I have been redeemed,
Bought with the blood and am now set free.
I am born again
Some day you will all come join me.

My mother did not fully recover from Kenny's death. I remember going with her to the cemetery outside Hawley to water the flowers on Kenny's grave. She spent an inordinate amount of time grieving at the cemetery. In all my ministry, the worst heartache is the pain of a mother experiencing the death of a son.

Kenny Quam

In October 1944 my brother Butch (then age 4) heard my father singing the following songs on behalf of my brother Kenny who just died.

Saved By Grace

Someday the silver cord will break,
And I no more as now shall sing;
But oh, the joy when I shall wake
Within the palace of the King!

(Refrain)
And I shall see Him face to face,
And tell the story Saved by grace;
And I shall see Him face to face,
And tell the story Saved by grace.

Someday my earthly house will fall,
I cannot tell how soon 'twill be;
But this I know–my All in All
Has now a place in heav'n for me. (Refrain)

Someday, when fades the golden sun
Beneath the rosy tinted west.
My blessed Lord will say, "Well Done!"
And I shall enter into rest. (Refrain)

Someday till then I'll watch and wait,
My lamp all trimmed and burning bright,
That when my Savior opes the gate,
My soul to Hm may take its flight. (Refrain)
~ By Fanny J. Crosby

No Night There

In the land of fadeless day
Lies the city foursquare
It shall never pass away
And there is no night there

(Chorus)
God shall wipe away all tears
There's no death, no pain, nor fears
And they count not time by years
For there is no night there.
All the gates of pearl are made

In the city foursquare
All the streets with gold are laid
And there is no night there (chorus)

And the gates shall never close
To the City foursquare
There life's crystal river flows
And there is no night there (chorus)

There they need no sunshine bright
In that city foursquare
For the Lamb is all the light
And there is no night there (chorus)
~By John R. Clements

In the Sweet By and By

There's a land that is fairer than day,
And by faith we can see it afar;
For the Father waits over the way
To prepare us a dwelling place there.

Refrain:
In the sweet by and by,
We shall meet on that beautiful shore;
In the sweet by and by,
We shall meet on that beautiful shore.

We shall sing on that beautiful shore
The melodious songs of the blessed;
And our spirits shall sorrow no more,
Not a sigh for the blessing of rest. (Refrain)

To our bountiful Father above,
We will offer our tribute of praise
For the glorious gift of His love
And the blessings that hallow our days. (Refrain)
~By Sanford F. Bennett

My brother Kenny was interrupted by God when he suffered a brain injury while practicing football.

DAVID JERNANDER

I received Jesus Christ as Lord and Savior in the year 2002. Before making Him Lord of my life, I was a very angry and bitter man. I held grudges against people that spanned over a period of twenty years without resolution. While I had the desire to forgive and move on in my life, I was unable to do so. The consequences of my unwillingness to forgive, and the inability to do so by the power of the flesh resulted in depression and anxiety.

One day my wife noticed that there was an **Alpha course** being offered in our local church. I very reluctantly agreed to attend this church function with her. We completed the course and attended the retreat at the end of the course. During the Alpha retreat there were several prayer stations throughout the community room, and one of them happened to be a forgiveness prayer station, which my wife encouraged me to go to. After much debate, I agreed. I explained my inability to forgive and I was prayed for. As the evening wore on, the weight of where these prayer ministers placed their hands on me got heavier and eventually led to a burning sensation. I did not realize at the time that this was the work of the Holy Spirit in my life. After three days this burning sensation ceased, and I was freed from this bondage I had lived in for so long. It was at this point in my life that I received Jesus Christ as Lord and Savior.

Before becoming a Christian, I had heard some of my Christian friends throughout the years say that God speaks to them. I thought these people were crazy and I avoided them for what I thought were justifiable reasons. After all, the fact that God speaks to people was a thing of the Biblical times, and I thought that such a thing could never occur today under any circumstances. However, I would soon find out for myself that God really does speak to people today, and now I'm the one who is crazy!

In the fall of 2003 I was laid off from my job. With little or nothing to do I decided to immerse myself in God's Word. I didn't really understand what I was reading but I did enjoy my time with the Lord. One day I got a call from the senior pastor of my church and he asked me if I would be willing to do a teaching for the upcoming Alpha course. Not knowing what I was getting into I said yes without thinking about it. Afterwards, I began to worry; what was I going to talk about? What could I possibly teach these people? I immediately turned to God in prayer. I was helpless and hopeless, and I had no real Biblical knowledge. For whatever reason, I began to look at Matthew 5:13–16 concerning the "Salt and Light," and I began typing away on the keyboard without any understanding as to what I was writing.

When the day arrived for me to do my teaching I was a nervous wreck, "I'm no public speaker" I said to myself. The closer it approached to my turn at the pulpit, the more nervous I felt. I finally realized my limitations, and turned to God in prayer for help. I said, "Lord, I' doing this for you, please still my nerves and help me through this." When it was finally my turn, I felt a sudden calmness come over me and the words began to flow through me. I was amazed at the results. After the teaching was complete my pastor came up to me and said, "Man, you were awesome!" I told him that I didn't think I was that good considering how nervous I was. He then asked all those in attendance, "Did you notice if he was nervous or not?" They all replied, "No."

When there was a moment of recess during the teachings, my wife who witnessed this incredible event said to me, "Honey, did you ever think about becoming a pastor?" I said, "No." She thought I should look into it. Not much longer after this another woman who heard my teaching also asked me, "David, did you ever think about becoming a pastor?" Again, I said, "No." I didn't put any more thought into the events of this day until some strange circumstances presented themselves coming from some unusual sources.

My wife and I were visiting with my sister; and something unusual happened during the course of our conversation. My sister out of nowhere said, "David, did you ever think about becoming a pastor?" I was rather dumbfounded and simply said, "No." This, however, generated quite a conversation between my wife and sister my teaching experience, and people questioning whether I'd consider becoming a pastor. About a month later, I met my friend Don for breakfast one Saturday morning. Don never had much interest in church or spiritual things. While we were enjoying our meal, Don said to me, "David, did you ever think about becoming a pastor?" Suddenly I remembered a story in the Bible I read when I was a little boy; it was the story of Samuel who thought Eli was calling him, only to be informed by Eli that it was actually the Lord Himself who was calling Samuel. I realized that God was actually speaking to me through other people and calling me into the field of ministry.

When I got home, I spoke with my wife about what happened at breakfast with Don. We began to reminisce about the events of the past concerning people who were asking me about a career in ministry, including my wife who was the first to notice my ability to speak publically. I didn't want to jump to any conclusions so I took a spiritual gifts assessment test to determine what my gifts were. I thought I would seriously consider entering the field of ministry, and I started by filling out applications for area Christian colleges.

After filling out the applications I prayed and asked God where He wanted me to go to school I didn't hear anything and I was wondering, "Did I actually hear God right?" In the meantime, I ordered some Christian books that would help me in my spiritual growth, and one of the books I ordered was by Kay Arthur titled, "Lord, is it Warfare? Help Me To Take A Stand." This book took me on a journey on reading the Bible inductively, and I found the process to be tedious at times, but rewarding. After two years of not hearing anything, I was beginning to get concerned. "Lord, why won't you answer me? Did I hear you right? Am I doing the right thing?" I wondered.

When I got home I started sifting through the applications that I filled out two years earlier, and sure enough, there was a completed application for Crown College which was sent off immediately. I was accepted by Crown and began my schooling in the fall of 2005. I graduated Magna Cum Laude from Crown College in May 2009 and I was a recipient of the Crown Honor Key.

David then went to Bethel Seminary and graduated in 2014 Cum Laude with a Master of Divinity degree and "Who's Who Among Students in American Universities & Colleges Honor."

David Jernander was interrupted by God by taking the Alpha course and went on to complete nine years of schooling.

CHAPTER 4

HISTORY
OF THE MENNONITES

The history of the Mennonites is another example of being interrupted by God. The Mennonites grew out of the Anabaptist movement when a Catholic priest began to carefully examine the Scripture.

Adeline Schmidt Dahlmen teacher, musician and historian is the daughter of Jacob Schmidt who led my father, Andrew Quam, to the Lord in 1936.

The following is from the book: The Schmidt Saga: One Pioneer Family (Ukraine to America) written by Adeline Schmidt Dahlmen. It is reprinted with her permission.

THE MENNONITE HERITAGE

Haven't we all at one time or another wondered where our ancestors came from and what events shaped their lives? This saga traces the history from the sixteenth century to the present of a SCHMIDT family origination in the Netherlands. This family has roots in a group with particularly strong religious convictions, the Mennonites. But who are the Mennonites?

Our SCHMIDT ancestors belonged to the Anabaptists, a group originating in Switzerland, who formed part of the Reformation movement sweeping Europe in the sixteenth century. These believers met in homes for Bible study and their numbers increased rapidly. They proclaimed their faith by being baptized even though they had had this rite as infants. Thus they were called "Anabaptists" – re–baptizers. They believed in separation of church and state, in rejecting violence and war (would not use weapons even in self–defense) and in obedience to civil authorities except in religious matters. This was then a stance against the authority of both church and state, and in 1529 Anabaptists were outlawed and were under orders of death. The only alternative to martyrdom was to flee; some Anabaptists did flee to other parts of Europe, including Holland.

Menno Simmons, a leader of one group of Anabaptists, was born in West Friesland, Holland, about 1496. He was educated for the Roman Catholic priesthood and began serving when he was 28 years old. Of his first charge he wrote, "I had not touched (the Scriptures) during my life for I feared they would mislead me. Behold, such a stupid preacher was I for nearly two years. . .At length I resolved that I would examine the New Testament actively."

The beheading of an Anabaptist led Menno Simmons to further thinking. When some representatives of the Anabaptists from Muenster, Germany, came to his vicinity and had gained a considerable following, about three hundred of them were attacked by the authorities and most of the three hundred were executed including a brother Menno Simons. Of this experience Menno Simons says, "After this had transpired, the blood of the slain, although it was shed in error, grieved me so sorely that I could not endure it. I could find no rest in my soul. I reflected upon my carnal, sinful life, my hypocritical doctrine and idolatry, in which I appeared daily under the appearance of godliness...I thought to my self, "I, miserable man; what shall I do?" This experience led him to a deeper examination of himself. He renounced the Catholic priesthood in 1536, was re–baptized and ordained a Anabaptist elder. About a year later, some younger men of high character, six or eight in number, came to him to ask him to become their leader. After careful consideration, he accepted the call.

Six years after Menno Simons had left the Roman Catholic Church, a decree was issued forbidding anyone to help him and offering a sum of money for his capture. After this he saw very few day of safety. **He spent the next 20 years in hiding, but studied, wrote and counseled groups of Anabaptists and their leaders.** He emphasized the belief in non–resistance and civil obedience except in matters of faith and conscience. His influence resulted in many northern European Anabaptists becoming know as Mennonites.

The nature of the persecution against the Anabaptists may be seen from the orders issued by the authorities:

1. No one was to ask pardon for them after they had been condemned to death.

2. Anyone giving information leading to the capture of an Anabaptist was to receive one–third of his possessions.

3. No one might conceal things belonging to them.

4. Anyone taken as an Anabaptist was to be killed.

5. All anabaptized children were to be baptized and their names given to the Roman Catholic priest of the respective parish.

When the Duke of Alba was made governor during Spain's domination of the Netherlands, wholesale condemnations were made and public executioners were busily engaged in putting heretics and rebels to death and seizing their property. **Alba boasted that during his reign of six years, he had put to death 18,600 persons of whom 1,500 were Anabaptists.**

Some were burned alive at the stake; some were strangled and drowned in rivers and lades; many were secured in coffins and buried alive; some were hanged by their thumbs and weights fastened to their feet; others, to keep them from praying or speaking, had their tongues burned with red–hot irons. One hundred twenty–five years after Menno Simons' death the book, <u>Martyrs' Mirror</u>, was published by van Braght, and Amsterdam pastor. It recounts the martyrdom of 800 Anabaptists; this book and a hymnal were carried by Mennonites of succeeding generations as they fled to safety.

It was in those days of persecution that a man by the name of SCHMIDT (first name unknown) fled from Holland to Moravia where Maximilian II (reigned 1564–1576) did not disturb the Protestants. Many Anabaptists found refuge on the estates of noblemen who were sympathetic. However, during the reign of Maximilian's son, Rudolf II (1576–1612), the Jesuits won back the country officially for Catholicism.

In 1585, this same SCHMIDT received word throuogh a friend that he and his brother were to be arrested that night. Hurriedly they packed their belongings and fled before the arresters arrived. His brother fled to France, and he, to Graudenz, Poland, near the coast city of Danzig. The Polish King, under whose domain this region lay, had granted liberty to settle there. As early as 1525, rumors had been heard in Germany and the Netherlands of religious liberty in Prussia. These rumors attracted many from various places to the Danzig region but the large stream of immigrants that came after 1530 were from the Netherlands, and most of these were Mennonites from north Holland.

Some of the Prussian noblemen, hearing of the work of the Mennonites in reclaiming swamp lands and building of dikes in Holland, invited them to settle on the lowlands of their estates on the Vistula River. At first they were laborers; later they became managers and then leased the estates for long periods of time. Eventually many of the estates became the property of the Mennonites.

Religious toleration was not a settled policy, but the Mennonites were granted this, among other privileges. They were, however, often hindered in the exercise of their religion and denied some citizenship rights.

Again and again, citizens became jealous of, and complained about, the Mennonites and demanded their expulsion and even the confiscation of their property. Fanatical clergy joined them in their demands. But noblemen and Polish kings, as a rule, confirmed and kept the promise made to the first settlers. This extended through the 17th and 18th centuries.

When Frederick the Great inherited the throne of West Prussia in 1740, the Mennonites of this area were well–pleased because Frederick had already shown himself friendly toward the Mennonites. A year after Frederick became king of this area, he promised the Mennonites:

- Freedom of worship.
- The permission to erect church buildings.
- Permission to establish their own schools.
- Freedom from military service.
- The privilege of substituting an affirmation for the oath.
- The right to enter any line of industry open to others.
- The right to bury their own dead in their own cemeteries.

But these privileges did not last long. Militarism in Europe caused the Mennonites grave concern, especially, when on June 20, 1774, an order was issued compelling the Mennonite congregations to pay annually, in lieu of military service, the sum of $3,500 for the support of the Military Academy.

After the death of Frederick in 1786, the new king, Frederick William II, was induced in 1789 to issue and edict to the effect that Mennonite owners of landed property formerly belonging to Lutherans would be forced to support Lutheran churches, schools, and parish houses. No more Mennonites were to be permitted to buy homes in Prussia.

For nearly two hundred years the Mennonites had lived in the Graudenz area near Danzig at the juncture of East Prussia (Germany) and Poland. They had acquired the German language and a settled way of life. But then, in the last quarter of the 1700's it was evident that both state and church were determined to stop further growth of the Mennonites. Hampered by heavy taxes, unable to secure new homes for their growing young people and to preserve their religious beliefs and family customs they began to look around for a new home.

For a hundred years the Mennonites lived in their settled villages under the privileges granted by Catherine II. Suddenly in 1870, Czar Alexander II decreed a policy for Russianization of the ethnic groups in the empire. Universal military service was inaugurated. The schools were to be controlled by the government with Russian as the language of instruction and control of village life would come from the imperial capital in St. Petersburg. This time they must move to a New World!

In April 1873, a twelve man delegation from the various Mennonite congregations left for New York to investigate the possibilities for emigration to North America. They visited Manitoba, Canada, and the states of Minnesota, the Dakotas, Iowa, Nebraska, Kansas and Texas. On their return the men reported that the Constitution of the United States guaranteed equal rights to all faiths, fertile land was available almost for the asking and railroad companies were encouraging immigration. The delegation enthusiastically endorsed the move.

Now it was decision time for the individual families. Sometimes the whole congregation or village decided to leave as a group. Passports and visas had to be obtained from the government and the Elder made a letter of transfer (attest) to another congregation. Maybe you have the one from your ancestor! Provision for food for the long journey had to be made – zwieback (biscuits) baked and roasted and meat cured. Bare essentials and the family's most treasured possessions were packed in a chest or trunk. Seeds of vegetables, fruits and, yes, the best kernels of wheat were included. They eventually would be the basis of the wheat fields of Kansas!

In late summer and early fall of 1874, the days of departure arrived! The twenty–one families who settled her were mainly from the villages of Michalin, Heinrichsdorf, and Karolswald, southwest of Kiev. They boarded a train to cross Europe for the port of Antwerp, Belgium; their destination was Philadelphia. Descendants of Mennonites who had come to Pennsylvania a century before had formed an Aid Committee. They contracted with the Red Star Line to transport Mennonites from Antwerp to Philadelphia where they were met and cared for until they could leave for the Midwest. The first settlers here arrived in September 1874, having traveled by train cross–country through Chicago, Dubuque, Iowa, and to Yankton, terminus of the railroad. A larger group of immigrants landed the last days of November, among whom were my grandparents, Jacob and Aganetha Schmidt and their year old son, John. A second son, Frank, was born two days after they landed.

Five families – those of Henry B. Boese, Fred B. Dirks, Rev. Cornelius Ewert, Rev. Benjamin P. Schmidt and Henry T. Schultz – claimed their 160 acre homesteads and put up sod houses that fall. What must their thoughts have been, having come from a village in a forested area, as they trekked the 40 miles across the tall grass prairie from Yankton? The other families rented a vacant store building in Yankton for the winter. Most of the men found odd jobs such as chopping cords of wood for 50 cents a day until they too put in their claims in spring.

In April 1875, Rev. Tobias Unruh, their Bishop in Ukraine, arrived from Pennsylvania bringing with him a gift of $300 for the congregation here. How could it best be used to benefit everyone? A yoke of oxen and a breaking plow were purchased; each family could have a few acres plowed so wheat could be planted for food for the winter. Water had to be carried or hauled from the Choteau Creek until wells could be dug by hand. Fuel had to be gathered for the winter – weeds, buffalo chips from the prairie, hay cut and twisted. Bishop Unruh also brought a loan of $2000 from which the families could borrow to buy tools and supplies.

Slowly, one year to the next, progress was made – more acres were planted. But sometimes disasters overtook them. In 1876 a plague of grasshoppers devoured the crop. In 1875 and 1880 two families lost everything to a prairie fire. Hail and tornadoes occurred then too to wipe out the year's labor.

Through it all, these 21 pioneer families were bound together in their faith. As soon as they were all on their land, they began meeting for worship each Sunday in the three largest homes – Cornelius Ewert, Abraham Schultz, and Henry T. Schultz. They were led by Rev. Benjamin P. Schmidt. In 1876, the group organized this Friedensberg congregation, the first Mennonite congregation in the Dakotas.

In 1877, when the oxen and breaking plow were no longer needed, the congregation sold them and used the proceeds to build a church; Rev. Ewert gave the land. Cottonwood logs were brought from the Missouri River bottoms, 10 or 12 miles away. Bishop Sprunger came from Cleveland, Ohio, for the dedication September 5, 1878.

But a church is not a building – it is the people. In conclusion I'd like to tell you what the ministry here has meant to my family and through them to God's work around the world. My father, Jacob, was the youngest of their 15 children. His mother, Aganetha, died when my father was 10 days old, leaving his oldest sister, Nellie, (then 18) to care for the family. His sisters told my father that Aganetha was a woman of prayer who dedicated all her children to God, some before they were born. God honored her prayers. <u>Of her 13 children who lived to adulthood, 10 became ministers and missionaries</u>. When Grandpa Schmidt remarried in 1898, and moved to Mountain Lake, Minnesota, Nellie was free to go to Berne, Indiana, to the Light and Hope Missionary Training Institute headed by Bishop Sprunger. There she met and married Henry Bartel. They left in 1901 for Shantung Province in north China where they founded the China Mennonite Missionary Society. Nellie might have been the first missionary from this church. In the next 20 years six of her brothers and sisters came to help in this enterprise. Three other brothers became pastors in this country. <u>Sixty–five years ago my father calculated the number of years his sisters and brothers, their spouses and children had given in Christian ministry. It totaled 897 years! No one has taken the time to add the years the grandchildren, and now, great grandchildren have served in Christian ministry around the world</u>.

Father Menno Sieman was interrupted by God when he carefully looked into the scripture.
(He eventually started the Mennonite movement that moved to the New World.)

Schmidt family members about 15 in number

Adaline Schmidt Dahlmen

CHAPTER 5
JACOB ALVIN SCHMIDT

JACOB ALVIN SCHMIDT

In 1936, Reverend Jacob Schmidt a former Mennonite pastor led my father, Andrew Quam, to the Lord.

JACOB ALVIN SCHMIDT

Born December 14, 1894 Avon, South Dakota

Died June 17, 1978 Cambridge, Minnesota

Married Annie Amanda Ewert September 19, 1919, Mountain Lake, Minnesota

Annie born January 28, 1897 Bingham Lake, Minnesota

Died May 7 1992 Cambridge, Minnesota

Account written by Dr. Ruth Schmidt a college president.

Jacob and Annie Schmidt lived lives which were a blessing to many people – to their children, to their congregations, and to their communities. Theirs is a story not unlike those of others of their generation and background; it is a tribute (as they were the first to acknowledge) of God's provision and guidance. It also confirms the belief that the United States of America has been, and to some extent, still is, a land of opportunity for immigrants. Certainly a third factor is the legacy of the Mennonite culture, of faith in God and an ethic of hard work and peace to all.

Both Annie and Jacob were residents of Mountain Lake, Minnesota as young people. Annie was born in the nearby town of Bingham Lake and Jacob in Avon, South Dakota. Both attended public schools there, but only Jacob graduated from high school. Since Annie's father died young, and she had an invalid sister, she did dressmaking as a young woman to help support her widowed mother. This skill was used to the benefit of her two daughters later who rarely had any "store–bought" clothes until they were grown. After 5 years of engagement, Jacob and Annie were married 9–19–1919, a memorable date in many ways.

Together they went to St. Paul, Minnesota, where they enrolled for two years in the Alliance Training School which was later the St. Paul Bible Institute, then College, and now Crown College. They completed the course there and continued on to Nyack, New York, for a third year of training for the ministry in the Christian and Missionary Alliance denomination. Although Annie had not graduated from high school, she had no difficulty in completing the same course of study as Jacob, and they graduated first and second in their class in 1923.

Both had to work very hard at a variety of jobs in order to support themselves and at graduation time had no money for their return trip to Minnesota. Indeed, they were down to a can of peaches and a few crackers for their own sustenance. As they attended a farewell for them at the little church which Jacob had pastored as a student, they were given $100, exactly enough to buy an open Ford and they, with another couple from Minnesota, who then could help pay for gas and lodging along the way, made their way back to the Midwest. Specific answers to prayer were often cited as they continued in their ministry for a lifetime.

As partners in ministry for approximately forty years, they founded churches for the Christian and Missionary Alliance. **Jacob never tired of telling the story of the big tent revival campaign in Mountain Lake, Minnesota, which led to the establishing of a church from which many young people went out to serve the Lord in the United States and abroad.** In Hawley, Minnesota, and Vermillion, South Dakota, Jacob supervise volunteers in the construction of church buildings. Together (although Jacob was the only ordained member of the partnership) they served churches in Waubay, Webster, and Elkton, South Dakota (a Baptist congregation); Mason City, Iowa; Fargo, North Dakota; Battle Lake, St. Paul (Hazel Park) and Albert Lea, Minnesota; and in Winter Haven and Ormond Beach, Florida, before retiring in DeLand, Florida.

Working with small congregations for the most part, and serving people who had little of this world's goods, the Schmidts were examples of servant leaders who used all the skills they had acquired because of their poverty and rural backgrounds for the benefit of people and the church. They had many talents; Annie was a very good cook and baker and it was a rare Sunday in which there was not company – visiting missionaries or evangelists of members of the congregation. She sewed clothes for her two daughters, packed missionary barrels, taught Sunday School, led the women's missionary societies, visited parishioners with her husband and sang duets with him as well. Jacob did all the things a pastor does – counseling, , preaching, evangelizing (many people were converted through his church and personal ministry) – but in addition he used his skills in carpentry, plumbing, wiring and car repair on behalf of the congregations he served and also went to assist female missionaries who were ministering to Native Americans in Minnesota.His skills as a printer enabled him to establish The Gospel Press and he printed over a million tracts to be distributed all over the country. He had his own printing press and set type the old–fashioned way. Jacob was also an inventor, patenting a baptismal heater and making tools, such as an edger, before these were available everywhere. No task was too lowly for this minister of the Gospel, but he always dressed appropriately to his calling when in public and sent his daughter Ruth to the hardware store for small items when he was in the midst of a job, rather than take the time to change clothes to go himself. Perhaps that is why Ruth still has a affinity for an old–fashioned hardware store where not everything is pre–packaged!

During the twenty years they lived in Florida Jacob first built a two–room cottage on property in Deland (one room for living quarters and the other for the printing press). This was their residence while he constructed a two bedroom home on the same property;

The cottage became a guest house where, over the years, they entertained dozens of friends and relatives. Jacob had a new hobby of gardening (raising two crops of vegetables a year) as well as several varieties of fruit and citrus trees. Annie filled the yard with tropical plants and flowers.

In 1975, because of Jacob's deteriorating health, daughter Adeline and her husband helped them return to Minnesota. The Schmidts lived a short time at the Eventide Home in Mountain Lake, Minnesota, before moving to the Grandview Christian Home in Cambridge, Minnesota. Jacob died in 1978 and Annie in 1992. They are buried in Mountain Lake, Minnesota. "For they were faithful." Nehemiah 13:13

Jacob Schmidt was interrupted by God in his attempt to be a missionary to China. How? By his wife becoming ill. As stated he was a faithful pastor and church planter. That is how he landed in Fargo, North Dakota and subsequently held 3 weeks of tent meetings in the town of Hawley, Minnesota "in the middle of town." He led my father to the Lord on the 21st night of the meetings. He consequently started a new church (Hawley Christian and Missionary Alliance). In 2015 it is still an active church (see picture).

Ruth Schmidt

Jacob and Anne Schmidt

Hawley Bible Church, 1938

Hawley Bible Church Present Day

The Great Revival of 1920 in Mountain Lake, Minnesota

(The following report was given by Rev. J.A.Schmidt, at the North Florida Ministerial meeting in Deland, Florida, March 12, 1968. After the meeting, a request was made by a number of ministers present, to have this put in print. Hence this report.)

I was the "black sheep" of the family for about ten years. Nine out of 13 children living of our family, were in the ministry; later I became the tenth.

In February, 1915, my brother Paul came to visit us in Mountain Lake and held some meeting in the then vacant M.E.Church. About 15 were definitely saved, I among them. Before he left, he organized a prayer group and asked me to be the leader. **We met in the various homes each week for five years, praying for revival.** From 10–20 and more at times, met in the various homes open to us. **Then in July, 1920, God met us in an unexpected outpouring of the Holy Spirit. We expected God to work, but not quite in such a community–shaking revival.** Two reasons may be given to account for this revival: first, The Mennonites are a religious people and many, perhaps most of them, had family worship in their homes and were faithful in attendance in Sunday School and Church, **Second: the undenominational prayer group that had been praying for almost five years for revival**.

Wife and I were married in September, 1919, and a few days later went to St. Paul Bible School. Toward spring of 1920, we became burdened for our home town and felt that we should do something about it. We talked about it to one of our instructors, Rev. Joseph Hogue, and he agreed to come as the evangelist. Our District Superintendent, Rev. J.D.Williams, agreed to send a tent and some canvas seats. After school closed, we went back to Mountain Lake. Several Christians asked me if we could not do something about the poor spiritual condition of our town. I assured them that I was arranging for some tent meetings, but asked them to keep it quiet to prevent advance opposition from developing.

The tent was erected in the city park on Saturday, July 17, in the middle of harvest. I borrowed the organ and pulpit form the vacant M.E.Church. Rev. Hogue came on Sunday afternoon on the 2:45pm train. The first meeting was scheduled for 3pm. The tent was filled for the first service and also that night. It was overflowing every night for

The next two weeks with 1500–2000 people in the park for every meeting. I had no experiences in leading singing or conducting a meeting, but in spite of this, God worked.

On Tuesday night Rev. Hogue preached on the Spirit–filled life. The 32–foot plank altar was filled with Christians seeking to be filled with the Spirit. God did not disappoint them either. Included among those filled with the Spirit was the editor of the two local papers (one a German weekly). It changed the editor, his editorials and also the content of the paper. I know because I worked in this printing office later and saw stacks of electrotypes of the American Tobacco Company, worth many hundreds of dollars in advertising space, which he refused to run. People from out of state wrote to inquire what had happened to him.

Mr. W.J.Toews, the editor, translated Dr. Simpson's "Gospel of Healing" into the German language and ran it serially in the weekly German paper.

At the tent, the 33–foot altar was filled every night and sometimes twice, with penitents. One night the message appealed specially to children. After the close of the meeting there were puddles of tears at regular intervals on the altar.

It rained three or four times during these two weeks, but never to interfere with the meetings nor the harvest. The rain came after midnight or before 5am, so the fields were dry by the time farmers went into them, to cut grain. The tent was a leaky one and since it did not look like rain when we left the meeting, we did not cover the organ. As a result the organ got wet and I went to the tent early in the morning and pulled out the valves and laid them outside in the sun to dry. Then in the afternoon I would replace them and the organ was ready for the evening.

All churches were closed for the two Sunday nights and cooperated in a measure by furnishing special singing.

Rev. Hogue had to leave on Tuesday to keep an appointment for meetings in Lima, Ohio, so Rev. Williams, our District Superintendent, sent Rev. J.A.Peterson and Rev. E.C.Swanson, both evangelists in the district, to preach each night till he, Mrs. Williams and Miss Sallie Botham, missionary to Africa, could come. On Sunday afternoon Miss Botham spoke under the anointing of the Holy Spirit with the result that the altar was filled with young people dedicating themselves to the Lord for full time service. In spite of a change in speakers, God continued to work night after night.

A conservative estimate is that 350 people were saved during the two weeks of meetings. The revival marked these young people. There was a spiritual wholesomeness and vigor about them that was unique. They were bold to witness for the Lord, specially in High School.

Money was no problem. We took offerings at each service, without pressure or betting. Al bills were paid and workers were well paid and we had $15 to start an Alliance Branch.

The new converts asked for weekly meetings. Since no auditorium was available, we met every Friday night on the lawn of Mr. and Mrs. P.P.Heide. Speakers for these outdoor meetings were visiting preachers who happened to be in town and also some local pastors. How these young people could sing and testify, for the audience was composed mostly of young people.

Before we left for our second year at St. Paul Bible Institute, we rented the Woodmen Lodge Hall, where weekly meetings were held. The Friday night meeting was discontinued and a meeting was scheduled on Saturday night and Sunday afternoon. This was done to accommodate the speakers who were mainly teachers and preachers from the St. Paul Bible Institute.

The High School young people organized their own prayer meeting. A little later the young people in the stores and shops also organized their own prayer meeting, which met on Friday nights. The older people and children met for the regular mid–week prayer meeting on Wednesday night. The children separated for their own prayer meeting after a brief Bible message. Thus we had four prayer meetings each week.

We came home for Christmas and right after Christmas Rev. Hogue came for meetings, which were held in the Lodge Hall. The Hall was packed to the door every night. Christians were helped and some souls were saved.

During the Spring of 1921, the Bosworth Brothers held a meeting in St. Paul, the Alliance Tabernacle at Midway. Some of the men from Mountain Lake, interested in the Alliance Work, attended the meeting. They took note of the Tabernacle, as to size, shape and type of construction. When we came back to Mountain Lake after graduation, these men called a meeting to consider a building program. They met in our apartment. The future of the work was discussed and it was decided to build a tabernacle 99x120 feet and to enlist the cooperation of the local churches so there would be a large auditorium which all the churches could use. But the churches did not cooperate, so in spite of this, it was decided to proceed with the building. Since our contract with Woodmen Lodge expired April 1, 1921, the services were transferred to the driveway of the Adams Lumber Yard, thru the kindness of its manager, A.A.Klassen. This involved extra preparation for each service, before and after the meeting, but plenty of help was always on hand.

On June 14, 1921, a call was made thru the local paper for 50 volunteers, 25 of whom should be familiar with carpenter's tools. By July the Tabernacle was far enough along to be used for meetings. Rev. Hogue preached for two weeks, but the crowds were not as large as the year before in the tent. Nevertheless the Christians were built up in the faith and some souls were saved. On July 6, 1921, Rev. J.D.Williams, the District Superintendent, came to organize the work. In 1937 the Tabernacle was dismantled and church building built on the same site. In 1965, a beautiful modern church building was built just to the west of the church, incorporating the first church building.

Mountain Lake has always been a fruitful place as far a Christian workers are concerned From 1870, when the town was settled by the Mennonites, till 1920, 100 men and women entered the ministry, an average of two a year. But in the next 40 years from 1920–1960, there were 250 who entered the ministry, an average of 6 a year. This is not an estimate, as I have the names of all who entered the ministry from the community. The first 25 years of the Alliance Church in Mountain Lake, 40 young people entered the ministry. The church has had students in the St. Paul Bible Institute (now St. Paul Bible College and Crown College) every year for 48 years, one year as many as 13 attended.

Among the outstanding events during the history of the church are the following: On June 15, 1922, Rev. Paul Rader, accompanied by Lance Lathan, pianist, preached two stirring sermons in the afternoon and evening. The Tabernacle was filled with people who had come as far as 60–75 miles. Rev. J.D.Williams accompanied them. Three days later, Rev. and Mrs. Luke Rader began two weeks of meetings. It was a wonderful time of refreshing for young and old believers and the Lord saved a good many souls.

June 13–18, 1933, Dr. R.R.Brown held a profitable meeting. The attendance was larger than during the Rader meetings and the churches of the community cooperated. The last service, on Sunday drew a crowd of 3000 people, so that loud speakers had to be used so those on the outside could hear. A large number of souls were dealt with in the basement auditorium. This auditorium had been prepared in 1921, where the meetings were held until the first church was built.

We give God all the glory, for it was He that worked thru His Spirit and brought about this awakening. By J.A.SCHMIDT

Jacob Schmidt's favorite hymn was "**God Leads Us Along**" as follows:

In shady, green pastures, so rich and so sweet.
God leads His dear children along;
Where the water's cold flow bathes the weary one's feet,
God leads His dear children along.

Chorus:
Some thro' the waters, some thro' the flood,
Some thro' the fire, but all thro' the blood;
Some thro' great sorrow, but God gives a song,
In the night season and all the day long.

Sometimes on the mount where the sun shines so bright,
God leads His dear children along;
Sometimes in the valley, in darkest of night
God leads His dear children along.

(chorus)

Tho' sorrows befall us, and Satan oppose,
God leads His dear children along;
Through grace we can conquer, defeat all our foes,
God leads His dear children along.

(chorus)

Away from the mire, and away from the clay,
God leads His dear children along;
Away up in glory, eternity's day,
God leads His dear children along.

(chorus)
By George A. Young

Mountain Lake Church and Missionary Alliance Church in 1937

Mountain Lake Gospel Tabernacle

Mountain Lake Christian and Missionary Alliance Church in 1992

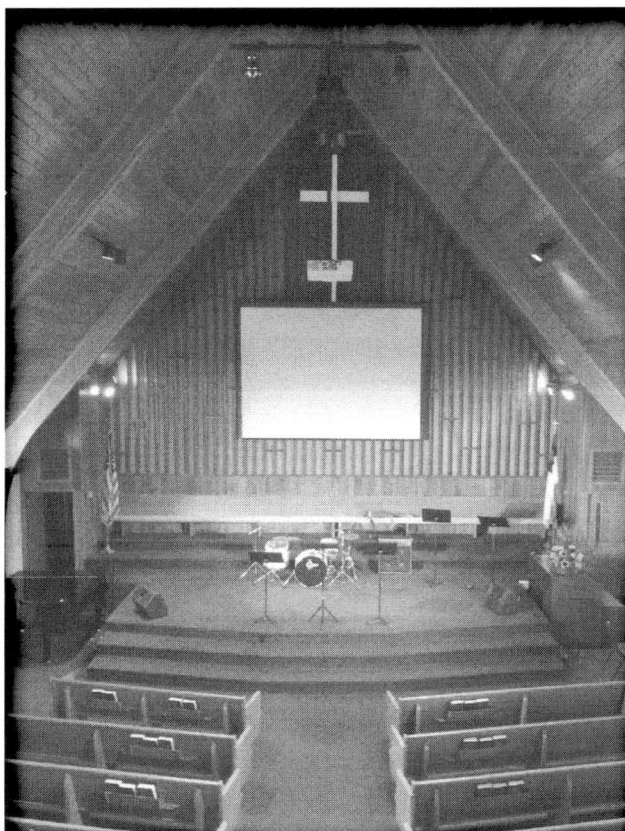

View from the church sanctuary 2015

Nairobi, Kenya
bdahlman@aimint.net
kdahlman@aimint.net

Dr. Bruce and Kate Dahlmen

Dr. Bruce Dahlmen is a grandson to Jacob Schmidt. He is a recipient of many awards including 2013 missionary of the year. **Dr. Bruce and his wife interrupted scores of his patients through healing, medications and care**.

CHAPTER 6

THE LIFE OF
ANDREW LEWIS QUAM

In 1972 my father was 75 years old. He was entering the three last years of life. My brother Butch decided to write a book "50 years in the Fur Buying Business" on behalf of our father. My father would record his thoughts on tape and my brother would write down his thoughts. My brother made 300 copies of the book. The following is a portion of the book concerning his coming to the Lord in 1936.

From "50 years in The Fur Buying Business" by A.L. Quam

Introduction to "50 Years in The Fur Buying Business":

This is the story of my father. It is not merely a biography, but an accomplishment in a life–long career in business.

His accomplishment in business was not one of obtaining wealth or some type of rank or status, but one of working hard at a job which he loved and which benefited the customers he and his business served.

His accomplishment was also of conducting his business in a Christian and ethical manner.

In the present day, when true business ethics are either non–existent or are practiced very little, it is reassuring to know of someone who had a set of business ethics and practiced them consistently.

Most of us remember reading about when Abe Lincoln walked four miles to return four cents he had short–changed someone. Well, I have a story similar to that to tell about my father. It happened when I was about 15 years old and was driving for my dad on his fur route.

It seems that we were south of Lake Park buying fur. As was usually the case, the trapper had an assortment of fur to sell – mink, muskrat, raccoon, fox, etc. It was during the discussion of prices, trying to determine an acceptable amount to both parties – that the trapper brought out a weasel that had been caught that morning. A price was given on the weasel to which the trapper gave his approval. Nothing more was mentioned about this furry critter, whose pelt was worth all of 75 cents, if that. They concluded the purchase of all the fur by throwing everything in the trunk of the car. Dad wrote out the check and we left on our way to another trapper several miles down the road.

Approximately four to five miles down the road, my dad suddenly told me to stop: "Turn around and go back to that man's place," he said. It seems that my dad had forgotten to include the weasel in the trapper's check.

Now it would be very safe to say that my dad was the only one who could have known that the weasel had not been included in the check. I surely was not aware of it and it is doubtful that the trapper knew of it since there was no item–by–item record made of the transaction. Even if the trapper did have knowledge of the fact, it could have waited until the next trip around to settle for the weasel.

But, we went back and paid the trapper for the weasel. (I remember the trapper had thought that the weasel price had been included in the total amount paid by my dad.)

Although I have never stated this story to anyone, it had a very indelible effect on my opinion of my dad and on the ethics which a businessman should practice. Two things describe my dad's philosophy of business:

1. Honesty in dealings with all persons – customers, employees, employer, etc., and

2. A sincere love for your work, no matter how humble or seemingly insignificant it may seem.

This book contains a collection of stories which were put on audio and tape and edited for printing. The events are all true (with the exception of some minor details which dad's memory, although fantastic at 75 years of age, may not be exact).

Although the title of the book is "Fifty Years In The Fur Buying Business," it includes items about the scrap metal, wool, and frog business. It also contains stories of his early trapping days, his boyhood days and his greatest accomplishment – that of becoming a Christian.

The purpose of the book was to collect at least in part the many experiences that have been told to me so that my children and others can enjoy them after he is gone from us.

~ Introduction written by Roger L. Quam from Sioux Falls, South Dakota

In 1920, the eye doctor examined me. He told me he thought I needed an operation. He gave me several x–rays and somehow determined that there was something wrong with a bone in my nose. So, I went to the hospital and the doctor cut out a piece of bone in my nose.

After the operation, I stayed at a hotel in Fargo. Each day I would go down to the hospital for treatment. In this manner, I didn't have to pay for high priced hospital room and care.

One night when I was coming home from a show, I walked into a Salvation Army street meeting. A man was preaching. After a while, they moved to an old store building where they held a service. I went to that service. At the altar call, I went forward for salvation. However, no one came and dealt with me.

For the next sixteen years, I sought salvation, without any help. I knew some relatives who had been converted, but they didn't help me. I didn't go to any place where they were preaching the gospel.

The doctor had told me that I had to quit using tobacco. Of course, it was hard. Every time I would have a sick spell and thought I was going to die, it did something to me. It gave me courage to refuse tobacco.

I got better and better and in about a year, I was feeling good. And then foolishly, I started to smoke cigars, one after another. In about six months, the same sickness came back on me. The doctor again told me to quit using tobacco. I quit and got well again.

In 1936, Reverend J. A. Schmidt held tent meetings for three weeks in Hawley, where I had moved a couple years before. I went to these meetings several nights. I would go until I got under conviction, and then I would stay home a night or two. During the last few nights of the meetings, I tried to hold up my hand during the invitation for salvation, but I couldn't. I just could not hold m hand up. Finally the last night, they sang the last song through and Brother Schmidt said, "I believe that there is somebody in the audience that the Lord is dealing with. I believe we should sing that last verse again." They did and when they got pretty well to the end of the verse, I broke and went forward.

I imagined that everybody was looking at me, that everybody was laughing at me. But, I went up there in the tent and gave my heart to the Lord. Jesus filled me with joy. When I came back from the altar, I didn't care if the President of the United States was watching me. I went home and expected my wife to be happy when she heard that I'd been converted and had given my heart to the Lord. She had gone to sleep, so I woke her and said, "Ma, I got saved." "Ah," she said, "You're crazy. Go on to bed." I remember I was so happy that I could hardly go to sleep. Next morning, I woke up and at first I didn't think about it. When I finally realized and remembered the night before – of getting converted, oh, what a joy came over me.

That morning, I was walking down the street in Hawley and two men were standing and talking. One of them swore and it just went right through me. Oh what an effect that swearing had upon me, now that I was a Christian.

After I got converted, it was hard for me in my business to tell the truth and conduct honest business. Many times, I suffered loss because I was honest and told the truth. It took me some time before I got adjusted and was able to always deal honestly.

Andrew Quam was interrupted by God when he accepted Christ that ended a 16 year search for God.

Andrew and Jennie Louise Quam with 2–year–old David

I was born November 29, 1942 six years after my father's conversion (my mother was converted a few years later). I had the privilege to be brought up in a Christian home. My father was 39 when he was converted. He had three brothers that were alcoholics. He had 13 brothers and sisters growing up on a farm near Glyndon, MN. He was a born businessman but he grew up without spiritual instruction. When I was born he was 45. I watched my father grow spiritually. He was unrefined educationally and socially. But I watched him grow spiritually.

"He greatly influenced my life."

7

WHO IS GOD?

The primary interruption by God was sending Jesus Christ to earth to die for our sins.

BUT WHO IS THIS GOD WHO INTERRUPTS OUR LIVES?

I'll never forget my oral ordination exam in the spring of 1976. It was held at Crown College in St. Bonifacious, MN. Eight men were on the examining committee. One pastor from Green Bay, Wisconsin asked me "David, who is God?" I don't remember exactly how I responded but I must have satisfied the committee.

I have often responded to the question "Who is God" 40 years later. Here is my answer.

The author A.W. Tozer says this about God, "What comes into our minds when we speak about God is the most important thing about you."

God has always been! He was before the creation of the earth. Before the galaxies, before the billions of stars, before everything. God has always been. He is eternal.

"By faith we understand that the worlds were framed by the word of God, so that the things which are seen were not made of things which are visible." *Hebrews 11:3*

"Lord, You have been our dwelling place in all generations.
Before the mountains were brought forth,
Or ever You had formed the earth and the world,
Even from everlasting to everlasting, You are God.

You turn man to destruction,

And say, "Return, O children of men."
For a thousand years in Your sigh
Are like yesterday when it is past,
And like a watch in the night." *Psalm 90:1–4*

"I said, "O my God,
  Do not take me away in the midst of my days
  Your years are throughout all generations.
  Of old You laid the foundation of the earth,
  And the heavens are the work of Your hands.
  They will perish, but You will endure;
  Yes, they will all grow old like a garment;
  Like a cloak You will change them,
  And they will be changed.
  But You are the same,
  And Your years will have no end. *Psalm 102:24–27*

"For My thoughts are not your thoughts,
  Nor are your ways My ways," says the LORD.

"For as the heavens are higher than the earth,
  So are My ways higher than your ways,
  And My thoughts than your thoughts. *Isaiah 55: 8–9*

For since the creation of the world His invisible attributes are clearly seen, being understood by the things that are made, even His eternal power and Godhead, so that they are without excuse. *Romans 1:20*

GOD IS OMNIPRESENT.

Can anyone hide himself in secret places,
So I shall not see him? Says the Lord;
"Do I not fill heaven and earth?" says the LORD. *Jeremiah 23:24*

GOD IS OMNISCIENT.

Oh, the depth of the riches both of the wisdom and knowledge of God! How unsearchable are His judgements and His ways past finding out! *Romans 11:33*

God is Omnipotent.

"I know that You can do everything,
And that no purpose of Yours can be withheld from You. *Job 42:2*

'Ah, Lord God! Behold, You have made the heavens and the earth by Your great power and outstretched arm. There is nothing too hard for You. *Jeremiah 32:17*

Then the word of the LORD came to Jeremiah, saying, "Behold, I am the LORD, the God of all flesh. Is there anything too hard for Me?" *Jeremiah 32:26–27*

God is Spirit

Now to the King eternal, immortal, invisible, to God who alone is wise, be honor and glory forever and ever. Amen. *1 Timothy 1:17*

God is Personal

Then as he lay and slept under a broom tree, suddenly an angel touched him, and said to him, "Arise and eat." Then he looked, and there by his head was a cake baked on coals, and a jar of water. So he ate and drank, and lay down again. And the angel of the LORD came back the second time, and touched him, and said, "Arise and eat, because the journey is too great for you." *1 Kings 19:5–7*

God is one in three persons.

The grace of the LORD Jesus Christ, and the love of God, and the communion of the Holy Spirit be with you all. Amen. *2 Corinthians 13:14*

God the Holy Spirit

The Holy Spirit is a divine person, underived, eternal, possessing all the attributes of deity and personality. He was involved in creation, He is active in the incarnation, the work of salvation and written revelation. About 25 ministries of the Holy Spirit are mentioned in the New Testament.

"But Peter said, "Ananias, why has Satan filled your heart to lie to the Holy Spirit and keep back part of the price of the land for yourself? While it remained, was it not your own? And after it was sold, was it not in your own control? Why have you conceived this thing in your heart? You have not lied to men but to God." *Acts 5:4*

JESUS IS GOD IN THE FLESH

Jesus said "I AM" (ego eimi) seven times in the book of John.
I AM the bread that gives life. *(John 6:47–51)*
I AM the light for the world. *(John 8:12)*
I AM the gate to the sheep. *(John 10:7–10)*
I AM the good shepherd. *(John 10:11–16)*
I AM the one who raises the dead to life. *(John 11:25–27)*
I AM the way, the truth, and the life. *(John 14:6)*
I AM the vine. *(John 15:5–7)*

God reveals himself in Jesus Christ. We would never fully understand who God is if Jesus Christ had not revealed himself to us through his Word.

"Therefore be *imitators of God* as dear children. And walk in love, as Christ also has loved us and given Himself for us, an offering and a sacrifice to God for a sweet–smelling aroma." *Ephesians 5:1–2*

How do we imitate God? By imitating Jesus Christ. How do we imitate Jesus Christ? By walking in love. What is love?

The Greek language has four different terms that are actually translated into the single English word "LOVE."

Eros   —   desiring, romantic, sexual love
             (this word is not used in the New Testament).
Philia —   brotherly love and the love of friendship.
Storge —   love of family.
Agape   —   is love which is of and from God,
             Whose very nature is love itself.

(It is the love that seeks and works to meet another's highest welfare. It may involve emotion, but it MUST involve action. Love is not spiritual goose bumps, but moral obedience. Love is sacrificially giving of yourself to others with no thought of return. Love seeks the highest welfare of another. In marriage, love is a total commitment to an imperfect person.)

The following is the list of 15 characteristics of love given in verb form, taken from *1 Corinthians 13*.

1. "Love suffers long." It is the capacity to be patient with the pressures brought about by the one loved.

2. "Love is Kind." It is the desire to bring about good to another.

3. "Love envies not." This refers to both envy and jealousy. Envy desires to deprive someone of what they have and jealousy wants to take it for oneself.

4. "Does not boast." Love does not vaunt itself.

5. "Love is not puffed up." True love is not proud.

6. "Love does not behave itself unseemly." In other words, love does not behave with bad manners. Love is tactful and does not embarrass others.

7. "Love seeks not its own." Love is not self–centered. Love is not pre–occupied with one's own interests.

8. "Love is not easily provoked." Love is not touchy or easily offended.

9. "Love thinks no evil." Love does not keep track of wrongs done by others.

10. "Love rejoices not in iniquity." Love is not happy when evil triumphs.

11. "Love rejoices in the truth." Love never overlooks, avoids, or compromises with error.

12. "Love bears all things." Love does not gossip. Love covers rather than broadcasts.

13. "Love believes all things." Love believes the best rather than believes the worst about other people.

14. "Love hopes all things." Love is optimistic. Love sees the bright side o situations.

15. "Love endures all things." Love endures things, not people.

GOD IS LOVE.

He who does not love does not know God, for God is love. 1 John 4:8

And we have known and believed the love that God has for us. God is love, and he who abides in love abides in God, and God in him.1 John 4:16

HE IS

He is the First and Last, the Beginning and the End!

He is the Keeper of Creation and the Creator of all!

He is the Architect of the universe and the Manager of all times.

He always was, He always is, and He always will be...

Unmoved, Unchanged, Undefeated and never Undone!

~Author Unknown

God interrupted me by being born. 100 years ago I didn't exist. "Before I formed you in the womb I knew you; Before you were born I sanctified you." *Jeremiah 1:5a&b.* In 1942 I was conceived in my mother's womb. November 29, 1942 I was born at 5:00 in the morning.

I didn't choose to be born. I received the gift of life.

In the late summer of 1949 I chose to trust Jesus Christ as my personal savior. I was almost 7 years old. 2 years later I was baptized.

You too can make that decision. No matter your age, God wants to save your soul.

Just repeat the following:

Dear God, I know that I am a sinner. I know my sins deserve to be punished. I believe Christ died for me and rose from the grave. I trust Jesus Christ alone as my savior. Thank you for the forgiveness and everlasting life I now have. In Jesus' name, Amen.

Then celebrate your conversion by being baptized and start to make other disciples.

POSTLUDE

Why did the Catholics hate the Ana–baptist and eventually the Mennonites?

Why did they behead them, burn them alive, strangle them and drown them in the river, bury them alive in coffins and burn their tongues with a red–hot iron?

Because they upset their church dogma and traditions, especially i nfant baptism.

In fact, infant baptism did not come from the Bible but became dogma through church tradition. Scripture offers no foundation for infant baptism.

Baptism (biblically) follows conversion. A person must be a believer before baptism. Baptism is associated with forgiveness, union with Christ and repentance. Baptism in an initiation rite into a believing community.

Verses concerning baptism:

Now when they heard this, they were cut to the heart, and said to Peter and the rest of the apostles, "Men and brethren, what shall we do?" Then Peter said to them, **"Repent, and let every one of you be baptized in the name of Jesus Christ for the remission of sins and you shall receive the gift of the Holy Spirit.** *Acts 2:37–38*

Then Philip opened his mouth, and beginning at this Scripture, preached Jesus to him. Now as they went down the road, they came to some water. And the eunuch said, "See, here is water. What hinders me from being baptized?" Then Philip said, **"If you believe with all your heart, you may." And he answered and said, "I believe that Jesus Christ is the Son of God."** *Acts 8:35–37*

Now a certain woman named Lydia heard us. She was a seller of purple from the city of Thyatira, who worshiped God. The Lord opened her heart to heed the things spoken by Paul. **And when she and her household were baptized, she begged us, saying, "If you have judged me to be faithful to the Lord, come to my house and stay." So she persuaded us.** *Acts 16:14–15*

Then Crispus, the ruler of the synagogue, believed on the Lord with all his household. **And many of the Corinthians, hearing, believed and were baptized**. *Acts 18:8*

Question:

Is the circumcised of babies in the Old Testament commensurate (equal to) with babies being baptized in the New Testament?

Answer:

Not all men who were circumcised in the Old Testament were saved men (personal faith). **Circumcision did not save in the Old Testament. Baptism does not save anyone in the New Testament.**

Baptism provides an opportunity to teach a new Christian the deeper meaning of the cross. Submersion in the waters of baptism speaks of the believer's identification by faith with Christ in His death and resurrection.

Water baptism is a public witness for the new believer. It is a graphic means by which friends and loved ones may see the significance of following Christ and the convert's commitment to Him.

To administer baptism to a new believer is to certify in the new converts heart the work of cleansing accomplished by the blood of the Lord Jesus Christ. The washing of baptism is an outward symbol of the inner washing of the blood of Christ. (Rev. Keith Bailey)

We are saved at the point of faith.

For by grace you have been saved through faith, and that not of yourselves; it is the gift of God, not of works, lest anyone should boast. *Ephesians 2:8–9*

But when the kindness and the love of God our Savior toward man appeard, not by works of righteousness which we have done, but according to His mercy He saved us, through the washing of regeneration and renewing of the Holy Spirit. *Titus 3:4–5*

Paul separates the two: "baptism" and "gospel."

For Christ did not send me to baptize, but to preach the gospel, not with wisdom of words, lest the cross of Christ should be made of no effect. *1 Corinthians 1:17*

How about *Mark 16:16, 1 Peter 3:21* and *Acts 2:38*.

Mark 16:16

"He who believes and is baptized will be saved; but he who does not believe will be condemned."

Mark is not teaching that baptism saves, he is teaching that unbelief condemns.

1 Peter 3:21

"There is also an antitype which now saves us–baptism (not the removal of the filth of the flesh, but the answer of a good conscience toward God), through the resurrection of Jesus Christ."

The word "antitype" means an earthly expression of a spiritual reality. It's a pattern, symbol and picture of a spiritual truth.

Peter is not referring to water baptism here. He is referring to figurative immersion into union with Christ. Just like the eight souls that did not perish in the flood. Water cannot save. Baptism symbolically depicts a changed life. Peter is referring to a means of safety from the judgement of God.

Acts 2:38

"Then Peter said unto them, repent (a change of mind and purpose that turns an individual from sin to God) and let everyone of you be baptized (the Greek word means to be dipped or immersed in water) in the name of Jesus Christ for the remission of sins (a more accurate translation "because of the remission of sins")."

The Great Commission

"Go therefore and make disciples of all the nations, baptizing them in the name of the Father and of the Son and of the Holy Spirit, teaching them to observe all things that I have commanded you; and lo, I am with you always, even to the end of the age." Amen."

Matthew 28:19–20

The Great Commission is: make disciples.

"Reach them"
– with the gospel (the good news that Christ died for their sins.)

"Beach them"
– baptize them (the New Testament follow up is baptism)

"Teach them"
– with the Word of God.

"I am with you always" – as you make other disciples. **Jesus trained the twelve apostles. Paul trained Timothy and Titus etc.**

"And the things that you have heard from **[Paul]** among many **witnesses**, commit these to **faithful men** who will be able to **teach others also.**"

Who are you pouring your life into? Are you attempting to fulfill the Great Commission.

WIPEOUT

Journey of a Stroke Overcomer

Pastor David A. Quam

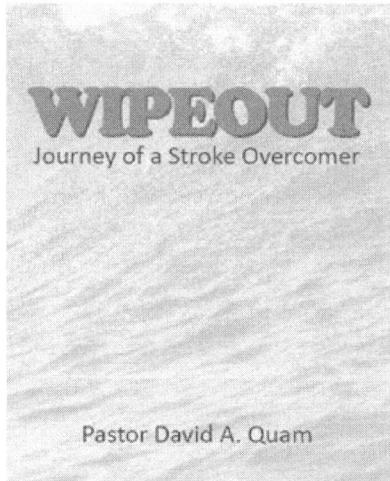

WIPEOUT BOOK ORDER FORM

Cost is $12.50 per book

(Price includes shipping cost)

Number of books ordered: _____ x $12.50

$_____ total amount enclosed

Please print clearly

Name:_____

Address:_____

City / State:_____

Phone:_____ Email:_____

Make checks payable to: David Quam
Please complete order form and mail (with payment) to:

David Quam
110340 Geske Road #228
Chaska MN 55318

Phone # 763-568-8772
Email: carolquam@yahoo.com

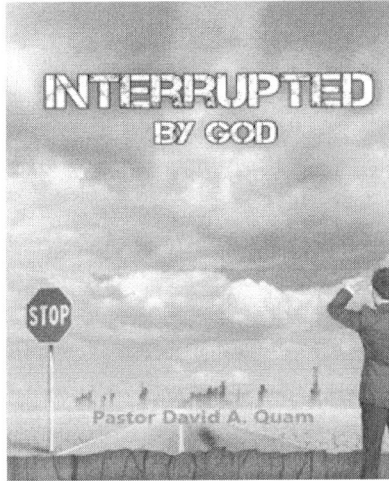

Interrupted By God ORDER FORM

Cost is $12.50 per book

(Price includes shipping cost)

Number of books ordered: _____ x $12.50
$_____ total amount enclosed

Please print clearly

Name:_____

Address:_____

City / State:_____

Phone:_____ Email:_____

Make checks payable to: David Quam
Please complete order form and mail (with payment) to:

David Quam
110340 Geske Road #228
Chaska MN 55318

Phone # 763-568-8772
Email: carolquam@yahoo.com